THE
Jade Coast

A familiar view along the Jade Coast is the coming and going of rain clouds. This one is in Chatham Sound, north coast of British Columbia, looking west following a squall.

THE
Jade Coast

THE ECOLOGY OF THE NORTH PACIFIC OCEAN

Robert Butler

KEY PORTER BOOKS

National Library of Canada Cataloguing in Publication

Butler, Robert William
    The Jade Coast : the ecology of the north Pacific Ocean / Rob Butler.

Includes bibliographical references and index.
ISBN 1-55263-513-9

1. Coastal ecology—Northwest Coast of North America.
I. Title.

QH104.5.P32B88 2002   577.5'1'0979   C2002-905857-0

The Canada Council | Le Conseil des Arts
for the Arts | du Canada

ONTARIO ARTS COUNCIL
CONSEIL DES ARTS DE L'ONTARIO

The publisher gratefully acknowledges the support of the Canada Council for the Arts and the Ontario Arts Council for its publishing program.

We acknowledge the financial support of the Government of Canada through the Book Publishing Industry Development Program (BPIDP) for our publishing activities.

All photos by the author unless otherwise indicated.

Key Porter Books Limited
70 The Esplanade
Toronto, Ontario
Canada M5E 1R2

www.keyporter.com

Design: Peter Maher
Electronic Formatting: Jack Steiner

Printed and bound in Hong Kong, China

03 04 05 06 07 5 4 3 2 1

*This book is for my parents, Cam and Doris,
who took me often to the seashore.*

*This book is also for Sharon, Holly and Myrica,
my fellow seashore companions,*

and for James, a new explorer of the shore.

A palette of colourful bat stars gather in Burnaby Narrows.

Contents

The waters of the Pacific reflect to a jade-green hue, Bischoff Islands, Juan Perez Sound, Queen Charlotte Islands, British Columbia.

CHAPTER 1

Land and Water

*It's in the air too, most noticeably when the great north Pacific low-pressure system
moves in and broods over the islands. The sea flattens like glass,
the horizon blurs in mist and rain.*
– John Broadhead and Thom Henley, *Islands at the Edge*[1]

*There is the great and quiet water
Reaching to Asia, and in an hour or so
The still stars will show over it but I am quieter
Inside than even the ocean or the stars*
– Robinson Jeffers, *Not Man Apart*[2]

A picture might be worth a thousand words, but a name can be worth a thousand images. The names Amazonia, Himalayas, Serengeti, Sahara and Patagonia all evoke a thousand images of the Earth's wild beauty. A lesser known but just as beautiful landscape is the Jade Coast, the verdant coastline along the north Pacific that stretches from northern California to southeast Alaska, bursting into a rich hue of jade green when the sun emerges from behind a brooding canopy of cloud. To the south languish the hills of California, the deserts of Baja California and the tropical forests of Central America. To the north lie the icy Bering Sea and tundra lands of western Alaska and Siberia. The temperate coastlines of Japan and Korea lie to the west, and the islands of Oceania sit to the south. These faraway lands are linked to the north Pacific through the creatures that roam both the distant seas and the shores of the Jade Coast.[3]

About midway along the Jade Coast, teetering on the edge of the Pacific continental shelf of British Columbia, sits Triangle Island, a treeless, windswept, sopping wet speck of land. Pummelled by howling winds, it is not a place where most humans would wish to be – unless, of course, you are a biologist.

The Jade Coast

Map of the Jade Coast

Triangle Island is the largest seabird-nesting island on the British Columbia coast.

I traveled to Triangle Island with three colleagues to research seabirds that made the island home each summer.

The island lies midway along the Jade Coast in British Columbia, where at latest count the coastal waters support over 400 species of fish, 161 species of marine birds, 29 marine mammals and over 6500 species of invertebrates.[4] There are more species of sea anemones, sea worms, amphipods, sea lice, shrimps and sea stars on the Jade Coast than anywhere else in temperate oceans. Aside from the number of species, the sheer abundance of some of these animals is staggering. The rivers of the Jade Coast support some of the largest salmon runs in the world and its estuaries and bays support millions of birds whose migrations span the western hemisphere. Puffins, murres, auklets, cormorants and gulls were on Triangle Island in numbers I had never seen before. In the offshore pelagic waters, whales from Mexico and Hawaii fed below albatrosses and shearwaters from breeding grounds off New Zealand and Australia.

If straightened, the Jade Coast's 85,000 kilometers (53,000 miles) of convoluted coastline would twice circle the Earth. Among the myriad of islands, fjords, and channels are quiet coves within earshot of raging tidal passages, and near-Mediterranean climates within sight of rainforests and mountaintop glaciers. The topsy-turvy landscape and contorted coastline is a mosaic of habitats with associated life forms that make the evergreen shores of the North Pacific a Shangri-la for the naturalist.

My three-week visit to Triangle Island brought into focus the abundance of life that lives along this marvelous coast. The rocks were festooned with sea life, the air was full of seabirds, and at night the sky was filled with sounds of nocturnal birds returning to their nesting burrows.

Thousands of technical papers have been written on the ecology of the north Pacific Ocean. This book is my attempt to synthesize this melange of reports into a single story, a daunting task that has taken over four years of writing. After covering some basic concepts in ecology in the first two chapters, I will introduce you to the ecosystems of the Jade Coast. You will travel far out to sea with the westerly wind. You will scramble along rocky shores, pick your way among boulder-strewn beaches, wade in eelgrass meadows and slop through mudflat ooze. Along the way, you will be introduced to some current, classical and contentious ideas in ecology and conservation of the sea and shore, and you will learn the common themes that govern the complex relationships between seashore creatures. By the end of the book, you will understand the basic connections of the major ecosystems of the Jade Coast.

The Climate

Sanity and madness are often close traveling companions. One only needs a near-death experience to see how closely they travel.

The day was clear and a steady breeze had grown into a menacing wind over the Strait of Georgia. The ocean was safe to cross when I shoved the aluminium boat into the water, but I knew there was little time to dawdle. The wind was threatening as I rowed beyond the shallows to where the 25 horsepower Johnson outboard could be lowered into the water. A few pulls of the starter chord and the engine hummed beneath a brief plume of blue smoke. I flipped the motor into gear and turned into the waves that rolled ashore. With the boat pointing toward deep water, I tucked a canvas tarp around my gear, checked that the ropes were secure and cinched my life jacket in place.

The run across the northern waters of the Strait of Georgia to Mitlenatch Island is often a blissful half an hour of boating. Indigo blue water and evergreen mountain slopes stretching to the horizon keep the mind occupied. But on this day, the sea had begun to move. A dark line on the horizon foretold of a fierce wind assaulting the sea surface a few kilometers to the south. Young men take to challenges with a purpose bordering on foolhardy, and I thought I could outpace the emerging storm. The throttle on the outboard was fully open when the first wave splashed my face. Within minutes the boat became briefly airborne. I was losing control. Whitecaps rose and dipped in lines stretching to the horizon. Land disappeared and reappeared behind waves. If the boat stalled, it would likely swamp and capsize. For an instant, I could see the lifeless body of the drowned man pulled from the lake during my childhood and the vain attempts to resuscitate him. The thought of ten or maybe fifteen minutes of consciousness before the cold grip of hypothermia snuffed out my life was enough to get me to slow down. I turned to see how much progress I had made from shore when the bow slammed into a wave, sending salt spray over my head. Soon I was wet all over.

One does not become philosophical in moments like this – instead, the mind becomes focused on survival. By riding up a wave, turning near its crest and sliding down the back, I could zigzag my way to the island. Soon I was gunning the engine up waves, cutting back at the crest and surfing down the back. "Turn, gun it, cut back, surf. Turn, gun, slow, surf." I found myself laughing maniacally at the waves.

The cries of seabirds flying about the island were swept away by the wind. Turning the boat northward, I veered into the lee of the island to seek calm water. I slowed the boat, took a deep breath, and stretched my cramped legs and hands. A few gulls flew by, feeling at home in the wind that had frightened the daylights out of me. Anyone who laughs at the sea will not be long on this Earth. Sanity had returned and I felt ashamed of my foolhardiness.

The rain and sunshine on the Jade Coast dance together around Mitlenatch Island. A southeasterly gale can swing to northwesterly in a few minutes as a weather front passes over the coast. The source of all this change is two opposing weather patterns that spar over the Pacific. When the Aleutian Low Pressure system dominates between October and March, the coast is deluged with rain and gloomy gray skies as a series of storm fronts swirl onshore by southwesterly winds. Opposing the Aleutian Low Pressure system is the North Pacific High, which starts in the south and brings fair weather that expands over the eastern Pacific Ocean with the onset of summer. It blocks the westerly flow of storms by shoving them northward, away from the Pacific Coast, resulting in the Jade Coast's fair weather and prevailing northwesterly winds in July and August. Many oceanographers and fisheries scientists think that these two storm systems are the regulators of sea life along the Jade Coast. The intensity of the winds is thought to control the rate of seasonal upwelling of cooler, nutrient-rich waters from the ocean depths, which feed offshore plants and animals and carry migratory birds to faraway winter quarters in Central and South America.

The west-facing slopes of the Sierra, Cascade, and Coast Range Mountains intercept the immense rain clouds hurled on to the Jade Coast by the Aleutian Low Pressure system for much of the winter. The west coast is known as the "wet coast" for this reason. The average rainfall along the coast is about 1500 millimeters (60 inches) of rain each year. About 1650 millimeters (64 inches) falls in Crescent City, California, but over 2300

Satellite image of clouds revolving around a low-pressure system. Image provided by ORBIMAGE© Orbital Imaging Corporation and processing by NASA Goddard Space Flight Center.

millimeters (90 inches) drenches Cordova, Alaska, and over 3200 millimeters (125 inches) soaks Tofino, on Vancouver Island. If all this rain flowed to the sea at an average rate per day along the entire 85,000 kilometer long shore, each kilometer of coastline would shed the equivalent of about ten Olympic-sized swimming pools of water per day. At peak flow in June, the Fraser River empties two Olympic pools worth of water every second! Imagine the immense flow of nutrients carried in freshwater streaming off mountain slopes that meets with other nutrients surfacing in upwelled seawater and you can begin to

Desolation Sound, British Columbia. In June 1792, English explorer Captain George Vancouver wrote, "Our residence here was truly forlorn, an awful silence pervaded the gloomy forests …"

understand why there is so much life along these shores. The enriched water becomes a medium for a floating garden of plankton, which is a source of food for fish, birds and whales.

The Sea

Hidden beneath its blue surface are some of the planet's most spectacular mountain ranges, with canyons that plunge more than six miles into the watery blackness. – Nathaniel Philbrick, *In the Heart of the Sea*

The Pacific Ocean is the source and sink of the region's rain, it moderates the climate on land, and it is a highway for marine life and human travelers. Other than waves that roll along its surface and tides that cover the beach, the ocean may appear to be unchanging, but this is not the case.

The Pacific Ocean is the largest body of water on Earth. It holds half the Earth's water and has a greater area than all the other oceans combined. Remove the water and the seabed reveals steep canyons deeper than Mount Everest is high, ridges and plains, submerged mountains, and flat-topped seamounts. On

14

average the seafloor is about 3,940 meters (12,926 feet) below the ocean surface. Nearer the British Columbia coast, the seafloor slopes gently upward. Extinct volcanoes known as seamounts pock the ocean floor, and others rise to within the sunlit portion of the ocean surface, where they become submerged islands inhabited by fish and other animals. Ridges from geological buckling appear in the seafloor about 800 kilometers (500 miles) from the coast, and less than 100 kilometers (63 miles) offshore, the seafloor gradually ascends the continental shelf. Here, the ocean water rising from the seabed converges with land-borne waters, creating one of the world's most biologically rich temperate regions. However, we need only to look at the diverse seashore to begin to understand the complexity of the Pacific. To do that, we must wait for a low tide.

While the Pacific Ocean is the medium for coastal life, the ebbing and flooding tides are its calendar. Tides bring food, moisture and organisms looking for a place to settle, and carry away the waste products, eggs and sperm of its multitude of creatures. The lives of so many sea creatures are set by the movement of tides that no discussion of the ecology of the Pacific Coast is complete without understanding them.[5]

Tides rise and fall in response to gravitational pull of the moon orbiting the Earth. By the time the Earth completes one revolution in 24 hours, the moon moves nearly one hour forward in its orbit. Consequently, it takes about 25 hours for a point on Earth to return to the exact position opposite the moon. This motion creates the gradual progression of the moon's phases from full to new. It also establishes a 25-hour tidal cycle in the ocean.

Oceanographers refer to one high and low tide in a 25 hour tidal cycle as 'diurnal' tide; when there are two high and low tides in a cycle, they are known as 'semidiurnal' tides. Jade Coast tides are a mixture of diurnal or semidiurnal tides. To make things more confusing, the high and low tides are uneven so that the lowest low tide follows the highest high tide. Moreover, high tides gradually become higher and low tides become lower for about a week, and then this trend is reversed.

Confused yet? There's more! The highest tides are known as spring tides and occur near the times of full and new moons. Neap tides fall intermediate to spring tides, when the moon is near a quarter. In addition to daily and fortnightly tidal cycles there is an annual cycle in which the lowest tides of the year progress from near midday in June to near midnight in December.

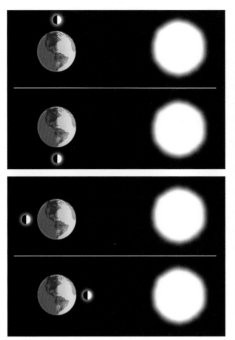

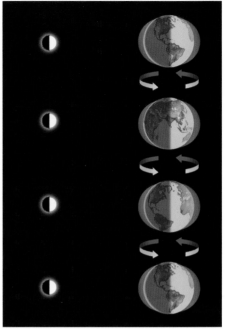

The orbiting moon creates spring tides when it is in line with the sun and neap tides when the moon is perpendicular to Earth and sun.

The tugging of the moon's gravity and the spinning Earth produce two high tides and two low tides in slightly more than a day. For a few days each month, the moon is perpendicular to the Earth's axis so that the high and low tides are equal. But on most days, the Earth's axis is tilted away from the moon so that a point on the Earth will experience unequal high and low tides.

Tide heights are measured from the lowest point they are likely to fall during normal tides. Canadians define this point to be the lower low water. The American system of measuring tidal heights uses the *average* of the lower low tides (also known as mean lower low water, or MLLW) as the reference point for the 0-meter tides. Thus, the American system includes so-called minus tides, in which the tide falls below the average of the low tides. In Canada, 0 meters is the lowest low tide, so minus tides are unnecessary. The amplitude of the tide is the range between the high and low tides and is about 3 to 5 meters (10 to 16 feet) on the Jade Coast. In both systems, tides are expressed in feet and meters.

The Land

On nearly every inch of land surface and throughout the fertile waters, life in varied form and function endows the Puget Sound scene with color, texture, and animation. – Arthur R. Kruckeberg[6]

On January 29, 1700, a massive earthquake flung a monster tidal wave over the Pacific shores, engulfing Native villages before roaring back out to sea. Deep in the abyss of the Pacific the energy of the earthquake moved westward, speeding across the ocean toward Japan where at 9:00 a.m., it sent another tidal wave to plunder Japanese coastal towns. In 1964 another earthquake that sent a tidal wave westward across the Pacific hoisted parts of the coast of Alaska 10 meters (33 feet) above their original height. On May 18, 1980, half of Mount St. Helens evaporated in an eruption that could be seen from space.[7] These were just the continuation of a long history of geological events that have shaped the west coast of North America. The Pacific Coast has been buckled, burned, frozen and crushed. Beneath the ocean, the Pacific Plate land mass is creeping under the advancing North American continent at a rate of about 3 centimeters (1¼ inches) per year. In our busy lives, we forget that continental motion is taking place beneath our feet until the immense pressure is relieved through erupting volcanoes and rumbling earthquakes.

There are thirteen volcanoes between northern California and Washington. British Columbia possesses eighteen volcanoes less than one million years old and five between five and 22.5 million years old. The Jade Coast lies in a zone encircling the north Pacific known as the "Rim of Fire" for its volcanic activity. Many earthquakes along the Jade Coast originate about 30 kilometers (20 miles) below the earth's surface off the coast of Washington and British Columbia or about 60 kilometers (40 miles) below the earth's surface near the Gulf and San Juan Islands.

Most of the mountain ranges and valleys in Alaska and British Columbia resemble large waves frozen in time. They get their shape from shifting continents and past ice ages that smoothed mountaintops and scoured valley bottoms. At the end of the last Pleistocene glaciation about 15,000 years ago, an ice sheet over 1 kilometer (two-thirds of a mile) deep smothered most of British Columbia and Alaska. Sea level was about 100 meters (63 feet) below the present-day level. Extensive lowlands reached 650 kilometers (406 miles) westward of the present-day coasts of Washington and Oregon. A few ice-free regions provided refuge to plants and animals on the Queen Charlotte Islands, in Yukon and in Alaska. With the melting of the ice sheet, the sea level rose and the land lifted from under the massive weight. Some fish were trapped in lakes suddenly cut off from the sea. Lands connected by ice became islands. Rivers roared to the sea laden with silt from beneath the melting glaciers. Wide deltas formed at river mouths, creating new habitats. Into this green coastal corridor

Humans on the Jade Coast

Trees along the Jin River become leafless after the frosts,
While my cotton sail is intact, working in the autumn winds,
Far flies a wild goose in the blue sky,
Slowly comes a lonely sail from the high sea
– Li Bai (A.D. 701–62)

We have come to think of human activities as foreign to the ecosystems of the world, as if we are recent aliens from a distant planet. However, human presence in the Jade Coast environment reaches back many millennia. The first humans arrived on the Jade Coast sometime after the last glaciation between, 14,000 and 10,000 years ago and hunted fish, intertidal animals, and marine birds and mammals. There might have been other visits from land and sea; Chinese and Japanese sailors likely visited the Jade Coast long before the arrival of Europeans. Chinese tradition tells of a junk setting out in 219 B.C. being blown off course and traveling for months to the east to a foreign land called Fu-sang. Hui Shen, a Buddhist monk, reported in A.D. 485 visiting, with 50 other monks, a distant land to the east that they called Fusang quo. Various spellings of Fusang appeared on European charts of the Jade Coast into the mid-eighteenth century, showing that the story was still alive centuries later. First Nations folklore refers to Asian visitors, and there are numerous reports of wrecks of junks on the Jade Coast.[8]

came animals and plants from the south and north, including the first humans.[9]

Today, the Coast Mountains of British Columbia and Alaska, and the Cascades in Washington, Oregon and California are a barrier against dispersal and invasion by plants and animals. The icy winter cold that sweeps across most of Alaska and Canada is held from the coast by a ridge of mountains lying northwest to southeast along the shore of the Pacific. A chilly reminder of the shielding effect of the Coast Range occurs a few times a year when icy blasts of arctic air spill over the mountaintops and blows through the inlets. For a few days or weeks, ponds freeze, snow falls in the rainforest and ice binds the mud-flats.

Freezing temperatures are short-lived at low elevations, but the tops of the Coast Range and Cascades remain covered in snow for several months each winter. On the summits, deep snow can be impassable to animals, and the cold can inhibit germination of plant seeds. Plants and animals that prefer the cooler and drier continental climate in the interior are unsuited to the wetter coastal climate on the windward side of the mountains. How plants and animals adapt to the interaction of wind, rain and sea is the subject of the next chapter.

Some of the finest wave-washed sand beaches on the Jade Coast grace the Oregon Coast near Coos Bay.

CHAPTER 2

Coastal Ecology

"Wouldst thou," so the helmsmen answered,
"Learn the secret of the sea?
Only those who brave its dangers
Comprehend its mystery"
– Henry Wadsworth Longfellow, "The Secret of the Sea"

When I was seventeen years old, I knew what I would study in graduate school. I would research all the ecological connections in an ecosystem until I understood why every plant and animal was present, and why some species were abundant while others were rare. I imagined studying all the connections between seabirds and the sea until I realized that this would take more than a lifetime. So I narrowed my focus to a small islet and finally to a boulder – until I realized that this approach would not do much to advance scientific thought. I was not the only one who had pondered the question: why are some organisms numerous while others are rare? This was a central theme in ecology.

The world would be much less interesting if plants and animals were evenly spread across the landscape. Mussels, barnacles and starfish cling to rocky shores, clams and soft worms burrow in mudflats, whales and seabirds are found in deep water. The conditions plants and animals must cope with in the open ocean are very different than on mudflats, which differ from rocky environments. These different conditions set the stage for the evolution of new species. Plants and animals that co-exist in patches share similar needs, but how numerous a particular organism might be within the patches is a complex story involving the organism's history, the presence of other creatures, and chance events.

Ecologists study how organisms interact with one another and their environment, pondering the patterns and conjuring up reasons to try to explain them. They refer to assemblages of plants and animals that regularly interact with one another and a particular environment as ecosystems (i.e., "ecological systems"). For example, organisms living at the mouth of a river live in an estuarine ecosystem because they interact with one another within the brackish water conditions at the boundary between river and sea. Ecosystems often contain several habitats. A river mouth, for example, might have stretches of mudflat, marsh and rocky shore habitats. Groups of plants or animals that coexist in an ecosystem or habitat are referred to as a community. Thus, the ducks and the marsh plants they eat are part of a marsh community. Along the Jade Coast are a few ecosystems containing many habitats and even more communities.

The Ecosystems

The boundary where one ecosystem begins and another ends is fuzzy because the entire earth is really one large ecosystem. However, here we will consider an ecosystem to be the living and non-living matter that interact in a particular region. The major ecosystems of the Jade Coast are the ocean, rocky shores, gravel and sand beaches, eelgrass meadows and salt marshes, and estuaries.

THE OCEAN

From any angle, the sea looks like an immense amorphous mass of water, because we can't see the ocean for the water. With oceanographic instruments, it has become clear that the ocean is made up of many different habitats, each with its own creature assemblages. Some regions of the open ocean are a soup of nutrients while others are watery deserts. Even more interesting is recent research that shows oceans are anything but stable. They are topsy-turvy ecosystems that regularly take abrupt turns.

While life is most abundant in nutrient-rich areas of the sea, seamounts are also rich in life. Some of the best fishing grounds occur where nutrient-laden waters rush to the surface along the continental shelf. But which species are present and their numbers are not so easy to predict.

ROCKY SHORES

The predominant substrate of the Pacific Coast is the rocky shore. It harbors a rich and sometimes bizarre accumulation of plants and animals. The types of creatures present on any rocky shore is dependent on their preferred mix of light, water, wave action, and the presence of other creatures. Calm shores of fjords and straits appeal to different species than the wave-washed, rocky head-lands of the outer coast.

GRAVEL AND SAND BEACHES

Wind and sea are forever intertwined along the seashore, and the waves whipped up by the wind cleanse the beaches of silt and other debris. Tossed and washed until clean, sand beaches are shifting habitats requiring unique special-izations among their creatures. Those species that live in the sand often are expert burrowers; those that are not move on and off the shore in time with the tides. Sand beaches are not common on the Pacific Coast, but they are more prevalent than mudflats. Superb sand beaches grace large reaches of the outer shores of Oregon and Washington, but in British Columbia and Alaska, they are more scattered. Fine examples are located between Hecata Head and Coos Bay in Oregon, around Cape Disappointment and Leadbetter Point in Washington, and near Tofino and Masset in British Columbia.

More common than sand beaches are gravel shores. Pebbles, gravel and cob-ble stones can withstand the currents and wave action that sweep away sand and mud. Beaches where waves tumble gravel provide little opportunity for plants and animals to get a foothold. But in sheltered shores where gravel is seldom disturbed, the rocks provide a firm footing for seaweeds, and the spaces between stones are homes for fish and invertebrates.

EELGRASS MEADOWS AND SALT MARSHES

Less than 0.5 percent of the coastline on the Pacific Coast is made up of mud. Mudflats are mucky places because they contain more organic material than sand – it is the organics that create the ooze. Calm water and low wave action allow fine organic particles of mud and sand to settle forming a footing for eelgrass meadows. Eelgrass meadows clothe the mid- and lower margins of mudflats, while fringing the upper margins of many mudflats is an assemblage of salt-tolerant plants that comprise the salt marsh. Plants inhabiting this zone can withstand temporary flooding during high tides and salt spray on foliage. Waving in the currents, eelgrass creates a rich biological ecosystem for many invertebrates and vertebrates. The long, green leaves of eelgrass make it an unmistakable seashore plant. Some large meadows are found in Puget Sound and southern British Columbia.

ESTUARIES

Estuaries arise where freshwater streaming from land meets the saltwater of the sea. Much of the Jade Coast would fit this definition in winter and spring but here the term "estuary" is applied to river and creek mouths. The flow of many creeks and streams along the Pacific Coast is too weak to influence more than the immediate region at the mouth. Moreover, many of the streams emanate from runoff following rains, so the flow is entirely a response to precipitation on the nearby land. During dry spells in summer, the streambed ceases or becomes a trickle, whereas during winter squalls, the streambed becomes a raging torrent. In contrast to small, local streams, the large rivers begin in the snowfields of the mountains. For large watercourses such as the Columbia,

Estuaries arise where freshwater spilling from the land dilutes the salt water of the ocean. This tiny estuary is at the head of Echo Harbour in the Queen Charlotte Islands.

Fraser, Skeena and Stikine rivers, the flow of freshwater is dictated largely by the melting of distant snow that often reaches a peak in early summer.

Food Chains and Webs: The Dietary Road Map

With the exception of a small number of species whose food energy originates from volcanic vents in the ocean floor, the tens of millions of species alive in the ocean today depend on the sun as the source of food energy. The sun is the engine of life on Earth. Over a century ago, Charles Darwin explained how individual plants and animals best suited to use this energy produce the most offspring.[1] Behind every species alive today is a history of successful lineages and failed experiments stretching to the beginning of life. The immense diversity of living things and the intricate relationships found along the Pacific Coast are the result of animals and plants competing for food and nutrients. Nearly every plant and animal is competing for its piece of the sun.

My breakfast this morning contained cereal grains from the Canadian Prairies, raisins from California, cane sugar from South America, salt from the sea, milk from cows in British Columbia, and orange juice from Florida. In each case, the food energy can be traced along a chemical reaction that began with the sun. Food is a packet of the sun's energy wrapped in a nutrient-enriched package. Plants are our doorway to the sun's energy: they store the sun's energy by photosynthesis of carbohydrates, which is released when we digest them.

In Pacific Coast ecosystems, the most important doors to the sun are tiny floating plants – the phytoplankton – followed by seaweeds and marsh plants. The phytoplankton generally cannot be seen without the aid of a microscope, but they are the basis of food webs in the ocean and the suppliers of oxygen for all life. If all the marsh plants and seaweed along the shore were dried and weighed, the total mass would pale in comparison with the weight of the phytoplankton along the Pacific Coast.

Ocean Thermostats

Phytoplankton are tiny ocean-going plants that contain chlorophyll, the chemical that plants use to convert carbon dioxide into food, using the sun's energy. In the process, oxygen is released into the atmosphere. Phytoplankton absorb large quantities of carbon dioxide from the air and sink to the ocean floor when they die. The concentration of carbon dioxide in the atmosphere plays an important role in the world's climate – high concentrations snare the sun's warmth, causing global temperature to rise. Phytoplankton regulate the world's climate by drawing carbon out of the air and depositing it in the depths of the ocean.

Plants manufacture food energy using the sun's energy to fire the chemical reaction – photosynthesis – that produces starch and sugar. Grazing animals, including humans, have essential enzymes in their digestive tracts to release some of the energy contained in plant starches and sugars, and predators have enzymes that release energy from the flesh of grazers they consume. Biologists refer to the route that energy moves from plants to animals as a food chain. Thus, a simple food chain is phytoplankton-zooplankton-whale. Tom Carefoot estimated that one adult fin whale eats 5000 herring, which consume thirty-five million copepods, which eat 4.5 billion phytoplankton each day![2] Food chains are seldom as simple as this because animals usually eat an assortment of foods. Some large whales, for example, eat shrimp and small fish in addition to plankton. The complex smorgasbord of food chains eaten by animals is known as a "food web." Food webs are our road maps through the ecosystems discussed in this book.

There are a few general rules about food chains and webs. First, food chains seldom exceed five steps from primary producer to top carnivore; in other words, orcas are only a few steps removed from plants in the food chain. On average an animal interacts with three to five other major species in a food web. The second rule is that the diversity of species generally declines along the chain. There are far fewer species of fish-eating seals than there are species of fish in the sea. The third rule is that predators tend to be larger than their prey. An exception along the Pacific Coast is the killer whale, which occasionally preys on large whales, but always as a group.

THE SUN AND MOON, AND THE DANCE OF LIFE

> *The sun was shining on the sea, shining with all his might;*
> *He did his very best to make the billows smooth and bright –*
> *And this was odd because it was the middle of the night.*
> – Lewis Carroll, *Through the Looking Glass*

A fundamental rule of the game of life is to produce the most number of offspring in a lifetime. Genes from those individuals that can most efficiently convert the sun's energy to create the most offspring that survive to do the same will have the longest tenure on Earth. Organisms undertake this task in a plethora of ways, reflecting the diversity of species. For animals that reproduce sexually, for example, finding mates is critical. Limitations in food, space and mates set up a competitive situation so that those organisms best suited to the conditions are most likely to reproduce.

The availability of food energy is crucial in determining the abundance, distribution and reproductive ability of creatures. If food energy is needed for growth and reproduction, and it is not always abundant, then creatures might time their lives to breed when energy is plentiful. Those individuals who fail to adjust will lag behind until they can no longer reproduce.

In springtime the marshes sprout new leaves, plankton blooms in the ocean and seaweeds become profuse along the shores. A green mantle of flourishing plant growth turns the Jade Coast a deep green. The consumers begin to browse the new growth and predators hunt their prey, and soon they begin to reproduce. In this way, the lengthening days of spring regulate pulses of food energy through ecosystems via plant growth. Many animals respond to changes in day length by scheduling their migrations and breeding seasons to correspond closely with the seasonality of their food. For creatures in the sea, the changing pull of the moon on the ocean becomes their calendar and clock. The rise and fall of the tides determines when intertidal animals feed and rest so their breeding seasons are set to lunar cycles in addition to the solar clock.

THE NEW PARADIGMS

When I was an undergraduate, it was taken as gospel that complex food webs were more resilient to perturbations than simple food webs. That all changed when Robert May showed that the opposite situation was more likely. May used some simple mathematical formulae to show that it was the strength of the interaction that determined the robustness of an ecosystem, not its complexity.[3] However, recent field studies have concluded that both views are partly correct – food webs are most stable when they contain many species and have a few strong interactions.

The resilience of food webs to major change seems to depend on the number of species that play similar roles. Food webs often have groups of species that do similar things, such as grazing on plants or preying on fish. The species in each of these groups might compete with each other but otherwise have few interactions with each other or those in other groups. The decline of one species in a group causes a close competitor's numbers to soar, and the more species are poised to take over in a similar role the more stable the food web.

Many people have expressed concerns that we are fundamentally changing the ocean's ecosystems by zealously fishing for large fish.[4] Here is something to ponder: we might surmise from our theory that food webs with the fewest species in similar roles will be most sensitive to exploitation and require strongest conservation protection.

Over the Shore and across the Hemisphere

When we try to pick out anything by itself, we find it hitched to everything else in the universe. – John Muir, *My First Summer in the Sierra,* Riverside Press, Cambridge, 1911

Many Americans consider John Muir to be the "father of the American national parks." His mountain wanderings led to impassioned early twentieth-century essays about conservation of high mountain wilderness. Of all the things that John Muir wrote, the quotation above is the most often repeated – and obvious to anyone who has given it a moment of consideration. The ecosystems on Earth are dynamic and recyclable, so given enough time everything will be hitched to everything else.[5] We know there is a great deal of interchange between ecosystems, and food webs are artificial constructs to help us understand relationships among species. The human mind finds it easier to comprehend complex concepts when presented in pieces that can be reassembled later.

Many marine animals travel farther in a year than we travel in a decade. Bald eagle chicks in eyries along the Alaskan coast eat a cosmopolitan diet containing fish scavenged from local water, ducks and grebes originating from the boreal forest, and seabirds whose lives began near the waters off British Columbia, Oregon and New Zealand. The homogenous distribution of industrial contaminants carried by seabirds along the Pacific Coast that originated in distant lands is a chilling reminder of the interconnectedness of all life forms. We forget this fact at our folly.

"To the happiness and prosperity of our Soviet motherland.
All hail the Soviet people. Long live the C.P.S.U. – inspirer and
organizer of all our victories. The ideas of Lenin are immortal."

This message in a champagne bottle, tossed into the sea off Kamchatka on November 7, 1976, was recovered on Anthony Island, Queen Charlotte Islands, on May 19, 1978.[6]

Champagne and slogans are not the only high seas exports that have come ashore on the Jade Coast. I have a collection of handmade blown glass floats that were used by Japanese fishermen. These floats vary in color from emerald to aquamarine and in size from a billiard ball to bowling ball. I have found these objects on rocky islets off Vancouver Island, on the Queen Charlotte Islands, on a remote island in southeast Alaska, and adrift in a channel. Each find brings a certain thrill. For some reason known only to beachcombers, these floats are valued above all other flotsam, perhaps because they were made by a pair of hands an ocean away. They also remind me of how things on the Jade Coast are hitched together across an ocean universe.

On December 9, 1994, a fire broke out in the engine room of the Hyundai Seattle, shutting down all power to the container ship just east of the International Date Line. Powerless, the ship turned broadside to the wind. Under the strain, cables holding the containers snapped, spilling hundreds of hockey gloves into the ocean and setting in motion a tale of castaways that would remain silent for more than two years. In January 1996, the first hockey gloves began to wash ashore on the west coast of Vancouver Island. They had inched their way across 3500 kilometers (2200 miles) of the Pacific Ocean at an average speed of about 16 kilometers (10 miles) per day. Pushed by the westerly winds, the gloves joined an oceanic wardrobe that has reached the shores of British Columbia, Alaska and Hawaii. One year earlier, over 80,000 Nike running shoes washed ashore between Oregon and Alaska from a spill near the International Date Line. Another spill east of the line sent a menagerie of toys bobbing across the sea; 29,000 blue turtles, red beavers, green frogs and yellow ducks rode the high seas to the shores of the Jade Coast.

The westerly wind that brings hockey gloves, running shoes, toys and bottled messages is the vital force creating the ocean environment that attracts to the North Pacific shores seabirds from the southern hemisphere, whales from Hawaii and Mexico, and fish for our tables. Our explorations of the Jade Coast begin in the next chapter where the westerly arises: far out to sea.

Millions of seabirds nest on the Jade Coast. Some nest on the ground on small islands, such as the double-crested cormorant.

CHAPTER 3

West to the Westerly Wind: The Open Ocean

Time writes no wrinkle on thine azure brow;
Such as creation's dawn beheld, thou rollest now
– Lord Byron, *"Childe Harold's Pilgrimage"*

From space, Earth is an azure planet shimmering in a midnight sky. The simple fact that most of the Earth is covered in water means that our planet appears blue in the solar system. Although we live on an oceanic planet, few of the sea's many features can be seen from space.

The sea appears a monotonous horizontal surface of amorphous, unchanging water, but nothing could be farther from the truth. Oceanographers have revealed that the ocean is a potpourri of regions with more abundant and diverse life than any place on Earth. And change is a constant in the ocean. Just when things begin to settle down, the ocean turns the tables on its creatures with sudden shifts in currents and temperature. The movement of water in the ocean determines the Earth's weather and climate.[1] The big El Niño of 1997–98 should have made that point clear to any doubters.

The Nuts and Bolts of Ocean Environments

CLIMATE

The ocean is capricious in nature, and marine plants and animals are regularly left scrambling to establish themselves in the new world order. Consequently, the players change every few years as a new set of creatures emerges to dominate the scene. Compare this situation to the terrestrial environment familiar to us

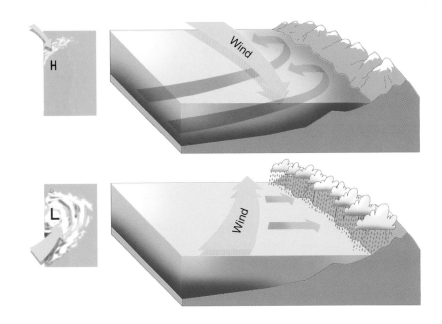

Ocean upwelling is a phenomenon that forms the basis of a food chain that links the lives of sea creatures from phytoplankton to whales. Winds blowing from the north or northwest out of high pressure weather systems and the turning motion of the orbiting Earth draw surface waters away from the coast. Cool and nutrient-laden water from the ocean depths is drawn upward to replace surface waters. The upwelling of deep ocean water slows when southerly winds emanting from low pressure weather systems push surface waters onshore.

landlubbers. Each year, small changes occur but, over our lifetime, the dominant players are largely still in place. It is not entirely clear why oceans undergo sudden changes, but it is certainly tied to the climate. Because of the fluid nature of the ocean, the changes cause a ripple effect that spreads across the hemisphere.

One of the most publicized shifts is El Niño. To understand how El Niño works, imagine viewing the Pacific Ocean from a spaceship. The tan coastal deserts, snow-capped Andes and emerald green Amazonia of South America lie to the right of the deep-blue Pacific. On the left lie the red deserts of Australia and the lush rainforests of Southeast Asia. As we descend to lower altitudes, we can see waves being pushed incessantly by trade winds from east to west. With the aid of an infrared camera, we can see that the water is warmer near Asia than off South America. Rain clouds deluging Southeast Asia rise near the equator to a high altitude before dissipating toward the west. The drying air circles eastward toward South America where it descends, parched and cool, over the Atacama Desert of Peru and Ecuador. We can make out the blue waters welling from the ocean depths drawn by offshore winds of Peru.

In most years, this circulating air remains undisturbed, but about every five to seven years an exchange of air between the Indian and Pacific Oceans reverses the trade winds near Asia. This reversal has a major effect on the world's climate.[1] The halting of the wind and the turning of the Earth push the warm water of the eastern Pacific slowly eastward toward South America, intensifying the unusual airflow from the Indian Ocean and triggering a slow march of rain clouds across the Pacific. When the wet, warm water collides with South America, El Niño is declared. In the winter of 1997–98, rainfall drenched the Atacama, sea level rose by 30 centimeters (1 foot), sea temperature soared 8 degrees above normal, and upwelling of cool, nutrient laden waters from the ocean was confined to the nutrient-poor warm-water layer near Peru. No deep, nutrient-laden ocean water reached the surface, triggering a collapse in the ecosystem off Peru. In the ocean of the Jade Coast, El Niño brought mackerel to the Washington and British Columbia coasts and deflected salmon migrations to the north.[2] The sea temperature rose 3 to 5 degrees and the sea surface by up to half a meter (20 inches). Sunfish, sea turtles and brown pelicans not normally encountered off the British Columbia coast suddenly showed up.

The effects of El Niño are short–lived, and the Pacific Ocean returns to former conditions generally in a matter of a few months. But some shifts in the ocean environment do not return to normal. In the mid-1970s, the North Pacific underwent a fundamental environmental shift that altered migrations and greatly increased the abundance of fish.[3] Fish born during this period began to dominate in commercial catches and pacific white-sided dolphins became widespread along the British Columbia coast.[4] Oceanographers believe that the sudden change was associated with a southward shift in an intense low-pressure weather system in the north Pacific. The intensified low-pressure system generated more winds, which subsequently drew more water and nutrients for the plankton, which are food for small fish that are eaten by salmon. A 2,000-year record of shifts in the ocean climate preserved in the accumulation of sardine and anchovy scales off California shows that the ocean's climate has shifted many times long before we started tinkering with the world's climate.[5]

Connections

Researchers in Europe have discovered an important link between weather and the abundance of many creatures in the Atlantic Ocean. The force of the westerly winds each year matches very closely the relative quantity of phytoplankton, zooplankton, herring and kittiwake breeding over about a 35-year period.[6] Presumably the stronger the wind, the more nutrient-laden water reaches the sea surface, fertilizing more phytoplankton and feeding more fish and birds. It is not clear if the weather affects each of these features directly each year or if the effect moves up the food chain from phytoplankton to seabirds. But there is little doubt that weather effects are so strong as to be felt throughout the marine ecosystem.

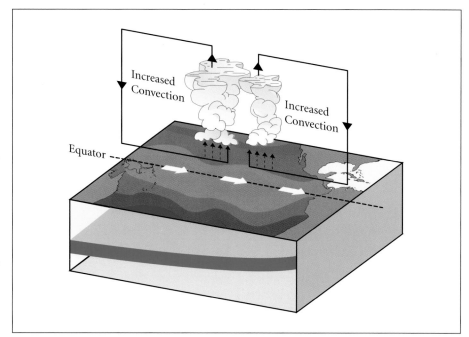

Surface waters pulled offshore by the combined motion of the Earth and westerly or northwesterly winds is replaced by cool nutrient-laden waters from the ocean depths. Plankton flourishing in this nutrient bath become the start of a food web that links their lives to most of the animals on the Jade Coast.

Winds along the Pacific Coast are caused by the low-pressure weather system meteorologists call the Aleutian Low. Satellite images of weather on television newscasts show the position of the Aleutian Low as a cloud mass swirling counter-clockwise around the eye of the Low. In summer, the Aleutian Low moves northward into the Bering Sea as a high-pressure system establishes over the north Pacific, bringing westerly and north-westerly winds and warm, sunny weather to the coast. The ocean can be very tranquil at this time of year. In winter, the Aleutian Low slides south into the North Pacific, hurling storms and rain along the coast.

Along the Jade Coast, from southern British Columbia to California, the ocean current moves southeastward, away from the prevailing wind. However, the water flowing out of Juan de Fuca Strait separating Washington State and British Columbia circles over La Perouse and Swiftsure banks at the mouth and turns to the northwest along the shore of Vancouver Island. This current flow changes over a few days beginning in October or November when the prevailing winds swing from the southeast. This is a signal that winter is not far behind. Upwelling ceases, waves become larger, and gales howl toward the Aleutian Low–pressure weather system in the Gulf of Alaska.

THE SEA

If the North Pacific Ocean were lowered a few hundred meters (few hundred feet), a wide coastal plain would emerge from California to Alaska with an abrupt step that would plummet into a deep abyss. This step in the seafloor is referred to as the continental shelf break. It drops over 2,500 meters (8,125 feet) about 30 kilometers (19 miles) west of the Queen Charlotte Islands and over 3,100 meters (10,000 feet) off northern California. About one-third of the way into the Pacific the seafloor lies over 5,500 meters (18,300 feet) below the surface.

The continental shelf affects the ocean's temperature considerably in certain areas. California makes us think of warm sunshine, but step into the ocean and you are in for a rude awakening. The ocean is unexpectedly cold, sometimes cooler than the waters off Washington and British Columbia. This is because cold waters from the deep ocean are drawn to the surface more strongly along the California and Oregon coasts than in British Columbia. The northern edge of California's upwelling zone reaches as far north as southern British Columbia. Cold-water upwelling from the ocean depths is especially pronounced between Cape Blanco and Mendocino in California, between Newport and Florence on the Oregon Coast and off the west coast of Vancouver Island where Juan de Fuca Strait yawns at the wide-open Pacific. Upwelling also occurs in passages between islands, such as Deception Pass in Washington and Active Pass and Seymour Narrows in British Columbia, as well as offshore where submerged volcanic seamounts deflect ocean currents upward.

Upwelling is created by the westerly and northwesterly winds blowing across the Pacific and the spinning Earth. Along the Pacific Coast in summer, the northwesterly winds blowing southward start a slow drifting current as deep as 100 meters (325 feet) below the surface. The spinning earth gives the current a rightward push so that the murky surface water moves offshore, drawing cool, blue water from below to replace it. This not easy to see – it is moving at a snail's pace – but its effect is felt over much of the west coast of North America. Thus the summertime westerly and northwesterly winds regulate coastal upwelling.

Upwelling water from the depths of the ocean creates regions of the west coast that are rich with nutrients for plant growth, which in turn contributes to the abundance of invertebrates, fish and mammals. Fishers know these places well. These deep waters carry high loads of nutrients – potassium, nitrogen and

Upwelling

There are four major upwelling areas in the world, all of which occur along the west coast of continents. The California upwelling region extends to southern British Columbia and produces about one-sixth as much biological material as the Peruvian upwelling region. The other two upwelling regions – the Bengeula off Namibia and the Northwest Africa (off Ghana and the Côte d'Ivoire) – produce an intermediate amount of biological material.[7] Anchovy, sardine, horse mackerel, mackerel and hake dominate the fish species in all four upwelling regions. Lying at the northern edge of the California upwelling region is La Perouse Banks, off southwestern British Columbia. In the early 1980s La Perouse Banks yielded an average of 6.6 tonnes of commercial fish per square kilometer (0.4 square mile) of ocean each year. This is attributable to a steady flow of nutrients in the upwelled water, which is enhanced by the Fraser River flows out through the Juan de Fuca Strait.[8]

phosphorus – the building blocks of life. Inland, freshwater streams are created by cyclones deluging the Pacific Coast. On average, over 23,000 cubic meters of freshwater enter the Gulf of Alaska every second, carrying nutrients from the land to the sea.

Sea Temperature

The temperature of the ocean in winter is about 10 degrees Celsius (50 degrees Fahrenheit) off Washington and 7 degrees Celsius (44 degrees Fahrenheit) off the Queen Charlottes. In summer, the temperature rises to about 15 to 16 degrees (59 to 61 degrees Fahrenheit) off Washington and 12 to 14 degrees (54 to 57 degrees Fahrenheit) off the Queen Charlottes. These are chilly seas – we would not last long in these waters – but in August the calm surface waters of northern Georgia Strait in southern British Columbia can reach a balmy 20 degrees Celsius (70 degrees Fahrenheit). Sea temperature plays an important role in dictating the migrations of salmon and marine mammals, the seasonal presence of plankton, and where seabirds nest.

For many sea creatures, the difference of a few degrees in water temperature can divide a zone of comfort from a zone of discomfort. Very distinct differences have been found in the distribution of Pacific salmon in water with a temperature difference of as little as 0.1 degree Celsius.[9] However, shifts in temperature might not affect the salmon directly; they might be tolerant of warmer waters, but their prey might not be so tolerant.

Ocean Food Webs

... the cells of life
Bound themselves into clans, a multitude of cells
To make one being – as the molecules before
Had made of many one cell. Meanwhile they had invented
Chlorophyll and ate sunlight, cradled in peace
On the warm waves
– Robinson Jeffers, *Not Man Apart*

The major food webs in the ocean along the Jade Coast begin with the plankton. The most conspicuous food web contains many of the animals familiar to us – fish, birds, and whales – as well as the plankton themselves. A second food web lives out of sight on the seafloor of the abyss, dining on the scraps of dead plankton and other creatures that drift into the deep. Some of the nutrients contained in this detritus eventually return to the sea surface, via upwelling, where they are absorbed by the meadows of plankton. Thus, the seasonal winds link the lives of surface and deep sea creatures and determine when and where the plankton meadows will flourish. A third web near volcanic sea vents relies on volcanic activity for its energy source.[10]

THE PRODUCERS: THE GREEN RIBBON OF PLANKTON
Much of the economy of the shore stems from the awakening of life in these marine "meadows." – Tom Carefoot, *Pacific Seashores*

Over a billion years ago, a single event changed life on Earth forever – primitive forms of plankton began to release oxygen as a by-product into the Earth's atmosphere. From primordial seas, gaseous plankton set the scene for the

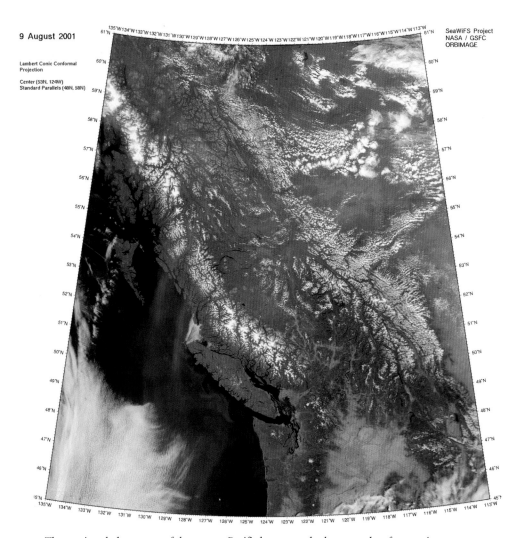

9 August 2001

Lambert Conic Conformal Projection

Center (53N, 124W)
Standard Parallels (48N, 58N)

SeaWiFS Project
NASA / GSFC
ORBIMAGE

The nutrient-laden waters of the eastern Pacific become a plankton meadow from spring to autumn. Plankton appears as a green hue off the coast of Washington and Vancourver Island. Image provided by ORBIMAGE© Orbital Imaging Corporation and processing by NASA Goddard Space Flight Center.

evolution of life on land and in the sea. Today, these tiny plants dominate the biological processes of the sea, and the growth of shellfish, finfish, marine mammals and intertidal invertebrates is governed largely by the flourishing plankton meadows in nearshore waters.

Yet when we look out over the ocean, it is difficult to see the pastures for the seas. From California to southeast Alaska, a floating green film of microscopic plants blooms in the strong rays of the spring and summer sun and dies in autumn and winter. When we look closely at the water we might notice tiny particles afloat but without a microscope we cannot see the teeming one-celled algae and tiny, unfamiliar animals. Infrared photographs taken from satellites orbiting Earth help us appreciate the magnitude of these meadows. They show the green chlorophyll of plankton meadows as bright red bands along the coastal upwelling regions from California to Alaska.

Plankton are mostly tiny plants and animals afloat near the ocean surface whose fate is largely cast to the ocean currents. Phytoplankton – "phyto" meaning "plant" in Greek – refers to the tiny plants among the plankton that absorb their energy from the sun and get nutrients from the surrounding seawater. Just like meadows on land, plankton meadows have grazers that eat phytoplankton and carnivores that eat grazers. These are the zooplankton – "zoo" referring to "animal" in Greek – which include a host of species such as larval crabs, sea cucumbers, starfish, and clams that later in life settle as adults on shore, and some species of fish. Like terrestrial ecosystems, the sun's energy is absorbed by plants, which are then eaten by animals that prey upon one another.

The waters of northern Puget Sound in Washington State and neighboring Strait of Georgia in southern British Columbia are among the Pacific Coast's most productive plankton meadows. The main species in plankton blooms are diatoms with awkward-sounding scientific names – *Skeletonema, Thalassiosira* and *Chetoceros* – and the major herbivores of the plankton are copepods with equally cumbersome names of *Pseudocalanus* and *Acartia*. The principal daytime zooplankton is the copepod *Oithona similis*; at night *Calanus plumchrus* and *C. marshallae* predominate.[11] These little-known creatures play a fundamental role in the ecology of the ocean.

In many parts of the world, phytoplankton blooms flourish for brief periods when the sunlight is brightest and rich nutrients are present in the ocean. Off the west coast of Vancouver Island, phytoplankton bloom in spring extends through summer, shored up by the flow of nutrients from inshore areas and upwelling in the open ocean.[12] They drift in the warm sunshine in a rich soup

The Tiniest of Plankton

Beyond the continental shelf, the open ocean is packed with tiny plankton – the picoplankton and nanoplankton. Another group known as the prochlorophytes are believed to contribute as much to food webs as the better-known plankton along the shelf.[13]

of nutrients, photosynthesizing and reproducing. However, this green ribbon of phytoplankton has more than its share of grazers and predators.

ZOOPLANKTON

The open ocean of the Pacific Coast holds over forty major species of zooplankton. They fall into six groups – krill (euphausiids), crustaceans (amphipods and copepods), chaetognaths, sea squirts (tunicates), jelly fish (cnidarians), and comb jellies (ctenophores). The most important prey for other marine life are the euphausiids, amphipods and copepods. The euphausiids resemble tiny 15-millimeter (3/4 inch) long shrimp that sport black beady eyes. At times, they are so numerous that they turn the water a pink hue. Often the actions of feeding fish and whales feasting at the water surface draw attention to the large schools of euphausiids.

More conspicuous and widespread than the pink hue of euphausiids at the water surface is the flashing green of nocturnal bioluminescent plankton. Nearly anywhere along the coast, the water sparkles with scores of brightly glowing dinoflagellates that flash for a few brief seconds. Then it is "lights out" until the next disturbance. On July 5, 1832, Charles Darwin wrote in his *Voyage of the Beagle,* "The sea was so highly luminous, that the tracks of the penguins were marked by a fiery wake." Darwin's observation might have been more than coincidental. Some recent research suggests that diving birds unrelated to penguins pursue herring at night by following the trail of bioluminescence.[14] The bioluminescence tattles on the presence of plankton-eating fish that then attract fish-eating predators such as grebes.

Many things eat copepods, krill and amphipods. These tiny creatures live their lives out of sight even though they are fundamental in the food chain of marine fish, birds, mammals and oysters. Copepod means "oar foot" in Greek in reference to their paddle-like appendages, euphasiid means "shining bright" presumably in reference to their bright red color, and amphipod is Greek for "water foot." The ubiquitous beach hopper that springs and scurries along our beaches is perhaps most familiar of the marine amphipods. The tiny copepods are about 1 to 4 millimeters (0.4 to 1.6 inches) long – about 1/300th the size of their relatives the lobsters. Two species of euphasiid shrimp are especially numerous along the continental shelf; *Euphausia pacifica* predominates in deep water and *Thysanoessa spinifera* abounds along the continental shelf. They spend their lives grazing the phytoplankton, diving to depths of over 100 meters (325 feet) during the day and rising to near the surface at night. Euphausiids, amphipods and copepods comprise between half and three-quarters of the weight in plankton trawls off the west coast of Washington and southern British Columbia. Zooplankton are abundant in April, very abundant in May and June and tail off through to September.

Another type of zooplankton are the jellyfishes. The quiet waters of Puget Sound and the Strait of Georgia harbor more than forty species of jellyfish, most of which are quite small and some of which are toxic. Their graceful motions, multitude of shapes, and translucent bodies make jellyfish seem innocuous, but packed into their alluring features is a deadly arsenal of stinging tentacles. The floating medusae is the reproductive stage. At this time, jellyfish are attached to rocks, wharves and the like, as hydroids. The most conspicuous jellyfish is the lions' mane jelly, resembling an enormous fried egg doused in ketchup. Streaming behind are tentacles that can reach 2 meters (9.5 feet) in length. The tentacles and lobes of this species are packed with stinging cells and should not be toyed with.

One of the joys of beachcombing is coming upon something new washed ashore on the tide. For the biologist, it is finding some new creature. A few years ago while exploring the rocky shores on the west coast of the Queen Charlotte Islands, I came upon hundreds of By-the-wind Sailor. This 3-centimeter (1.4 inch) long, icy blue colored jellyfish sports a triangular transparent appendage set to catch the wind. I had read much about these animals from accounts of sailors. Most species of jellyfish are prisoners to the ocean currents but the By-the-wind Sailor has taken advantage of the wind in its "sail" to move in new directions and at a faster pace than its brethren have.

Many other creatures can be found among the plankton meadows along the seashore. From snails to starfish, most marine invertebrates begin their lives as part of the plankton. The advantage of joining the plankton is that it is an effective means of pioneering new shores. As a general rule, species that remain in the plankton the longest disperse the farthest. The Sitka Periwinkle, for example,

The moon jelly produces mucus to trap tiny crustaceans and plankton, which it then transports to the mouth with the help of tiny hair-like appendages.

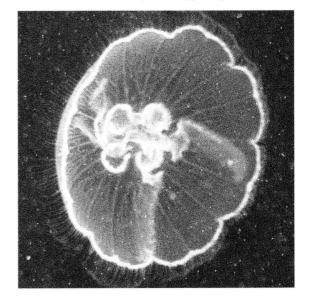

Guided by Earth's Magnet Field

The migrations of animals have intrigued humans for millennia. We have wondered how some animals can trek across the globe and return a few months later to the same place. There is now some evidence showing that fin whales use the magnetic field surrounding the Earth to navigate the world's oceans.[16] It remains to be seen how many other animals use magnetism as their cue.

is a homebody and has a brief planktonic stage of a few days, whereas its close relative, the Checkered Periwinkle, drifts for twenty to thirty days before settling down. Snails, limpets, chitons and mussels generally have short plankton stages of under two weeks, barnacles float for two to three weeks, sea cucumbers drift for up to nine weeks, and the purple starfish drifts for up to seven months. In California, some marine animals time the release of their larvae to coincide with the offshore flow of seawater to the "greener pastures" in the upwelling region of the coast. The larvae remain at sea until the winds cease in autumn and the onshore movement of the ocean currents carry them back to shore where they settle and grow into adults.[15]

THE DETRITUS

He sinks into thy depths with bubbling groan,
Without a grave, unknelled, unconfined and unknown
– Lord Byron, *Childe Harold's Pilgrimage*

During spring and summer the wind-driven upwelling feeds a flourishing meadow of phytoplankton and a community of zooplankton predators in the upper few meters of the ocean. Throughout this time, the dead and dying plankton fall and settle on the seabed. In autumn, when the winds start to falter, ceasing to generate the upwelling of nutrients, the shower of dying plankton turns to a downpour. The first indication of a shift in winds usually comes in September.

In some years, however, the prevailing winds swing from northwest to southeast in a matter of days, bringing the current along the continental shelf to a standstill. Upwelling ceases, nutrients from the ocean depths turn to a trickle and the plankton stop reproducing. Some of the plankton sense the sudden shutdown and retreat to the ocean floor to await the release of spores to repopulate the sea surface the following spring. However, most plankton die and their remains begin a slow journey into the depths. Few predators can survive in the cold waters on the seafloor, and this allows a large amphipod community to thrive on the abundant supply of detritus. Upwelling will bring up the nutrients from the seafloor when the winds blow from the northwest again the following spring.

PLANKTON PREDATORS

It was mid-summer, and the sun shone brightly as we rounded Cape Chacon at the southernmost gateway in the archipelago of southeast Alaska. I had joined friend and fellow sailor Randy Burke on an exploratory six-day trip in Alaska aboard the 20-meter (70-foot) Island Roamer. Randy spotted the first blow while we were several kilometers away. At first we thought it was from a humpback whale, which are common in the area, but as we motored closer, it was obvious from their size and speed that these whales were something new.

The fin whale is the second-largest animal on Earth after the blue whale and remarkably agile for its size. Some individuals reach 26 meters (85 feet) in length and weigh 80 tonnes (88 tons). The whales we saw at Cape Chacon were about 20 meters (70 feet) long. They were pursuing schools of plankton that they gulped into large expandable mouths, expelling the water through baleen plates. Baleen is a form of cuticle that hangs in shreds from the roof of mouths of filter-feeding whales. Plankton, small fish and water are gulped into the open mouth. The whale's immense tongue pushes the soupy broth against the roof of its mouth, expelling water through the baleen plates and retaining the plankton and fish. As I watched, it occured to me that these large whales were eating the smallest of prey.

Plankton-Eating Fish

Like fin whales, many sea animals eat plankton their entire lives; others are weaned on plankton before preying on fish later in life. Small fish such as herring, anchovies, eulachons and sandlance eat plankton throughout their lives. Other fish such as hake, salmon and dogfish eat plankton when they are young and small fish as they grow larger. One very large fish that has taken to feeding on plankton for its entire adult life is the 10-meter (33-foot) long basking shark. At nearly 4,000 kilograms (9,000 pounds), the basking shark is the second-largest fish in the world after another plankton eater, the whale shark. Both eat by swimming about in plankton-rich water with its mouth open.

Euphausiids are the mainstay of herring that swarm over the continental shelf in spring and summer. By October, some of the herring slip away from the banks for deeper water near the shelf along British Columbia and Alaska's coastline. Late winter finds them gathering once more over the banks in preparation for migration to their spawning grounds in places such as the Strait of Georgia, and Barkley, Clayoquot, Nootka, Craig Hoonah and Prince William sounds. Young herring appear to stay close to shore for the first year.

Another small plankton eater is the eulachon, known colloquially as candlefish or hooligan. It is a smelt that spawns in large rivers and spends the rest of its life at sea. It enters the sea from spawning rivers in late spring and returns to the outer coast by mid-summer. Anchovies can also be numerous in the offshore waters of California and Oregon but are generally scarce elsewhere. Recently, anchovies have made a bit of a comeback. One of the oddest fishes to inhabit the banks off the Jade Coast is the sandlance, a long, thin, silvery fish that forms into huge schools. The sandlance spawns in late winter and becomes numerous in offshore areas from spring through late summer. However, for the rest of the year, the sandlance is thought to lie buried in the sand.[17] Sandlance feed largely on copepods.

The major fish predators on La Perouse Bank are hake, dogfish and Chinook salmon, which forage on abundant herring and euphausiids. One estimate put the quantity of euphausiids eaten by these predators at 300,000 tonnes (330,700 tons) and herring at 35,000 tonnes (38,600 tons) per day. Dogfish also eat hake – 29,000 tonnes (32,000 tons) each year. The significance of euphausiids to fish, birds and mammals was witnessed by Dan Ware onboard a Canadian Fisheries research ship over La Perouse Bank on August 16, 1988 when huge schools of herring and dogfish, thousands of seabirds and ten humpback whales gorged on euphausiids and herring in a small area of the bank. Euphausiids are estimated to provide over 80 percent of the diet of about 342,000 tonnes (377,000 tons) of fish that spend the summer off the west coast of Vancouver Island, suggesting that the tiny euphausiids are the basis of this food web.

The most abundant species of fish that inhabits the upwelling area off the west coast of Vancouver Island is the Pacific hake. Most hake off Vancouver Island spawn off California. After spawning is completed, hake migrate northward, traveling at a rate of about 17 kilometers (10 miles) each day, arriving in May off the west coast of Vancouver Island. They gorge on euphausiids and herring as far north as Queen Charlotte Sound until late August when they dis-

The salmon are important transporters of nutrients into rivers along the Jade Coast. They become food for bears and birds, and their decaying carcasses release ocean nutrients into the river (Danny Kent photo).

perse to the shelf. They remain along the shelf until the winds shift in October and then return south.

More than any other animal, the salmon are the icons of the Jade Coast. The great salmon-producing rivers include the Columbia, Fraser, Skeena and Stikine, but many smaller streams and rivers contain genetically unique stocks of their own. The five species of salmon that occur in the eastern Pacific are the Chinook, sockeye, chum, pink and coho, and in the western Pacific the masu is abundant. Sockeye, pink and chum salmon are seasonal residents while coho and Chinook are present at all times of the year. One estimate puts the total number of salmon that migrate north along the shores of the Pacific Coast at about 114 million fish.[18]

When they leave the great rivers where they were reared, the juvenile salmon meet with others of their kind from Oregon, Washington, British Columbia and Alaska, swimming northward along the continental shelf and eventually westward into the open Pacific. The great swarms of salmon fan out in search of plankton and small fish drawn to the rich, nutrient-laden waters. Their travels trace the Jade Coast from California to Japan and north to the Bering Sea.

The salmon are thought to have evolved from a common ancestor that lived about eight million years ago. Glaciation isolated spawning groups, which adapted to local conditions until they could no longer breed with other stocks. The chum and pinks come to the sea as fry and stay close to shore for a few weeks before venturing into the open ocean. Sockeye and coho remain in lakes and rivers for a few years before bolting for the open ocean. Some Chinooks make a quick run to the sea like chums and pinks, while others linger in rivers for several weeks before departing. Still others delay their departure for a few years and in this way behave like sockeye and coho. Life is not easy for young salmon – mortality in the first few weeks at sea can reach as high as 10 percent per week. The departure of salmon from estuaries for the open ocean usually coincides with the peak abundance of their zooplankton prey in April and May.[19]

Plankton-Eating Birds

Out there, buried hundreds, even thousands, of miles deep in the spume of the storm, millions of them were riding the wind, fighting for their lives.
– Franklin Russell, *The Sea Has Wings*

Seabirds are among the most conspicuous of the ocean's animals. Nearly 14.5 million seabirds of nineteen species are estimated to nest along the Jade Coast.[20] The plankton-eating species are the most numerous. Almost one-quarter of the seabirds are Cassin's auklets and half are Leach's and fork-tailed storm petrels.

A few years ago, I was traveling along the west coast of the Queen Charlotte Islands a day after a fierce westerly wind had subsided. The sunny, warm afternoon was a welcome respite, and the seabirds on the water seemed to be enjoying the sun too. On calm days such as this, life on the sea seems to enter a dream state. I noticed two parakeet auklets popping to the surface like Punch and Judy puppets. Startled, they took to the wing and were out of sight in a moment. This was my first sighting (and the first ever in inshore waters in Canada) of a species that breeds on the Aleutian Islands, an archipelago stretching westward from Alaska.

Far more numerous than the parakeet auklet but also seldom seen close to land is the plankton-eating Cassin's auklet.[21] Hundreds of thousands nest on the Aleutian Islands and in a few places in British Columbia, while a few thousand nest in Washington, Oregon and California. You might be lucky and catch a glimpse of the Cassin's auklet from a rocky headland but to see them up close requires a visit to their remote island colonies.

Cassin's auklets eat the rich plankton found along the continental shelf of the Pacific Coast. They dive for food and carry it in a throat pouch to their young, which are hidden from predators in burrows that riddle the ground on a few suitable nesting islands. Euphausiids are among the most numerous items eaten by the auklet, but the most important by far is a copepod called *Neocalanus cristatus*. It has no common name, but since cristatus means "crest," let's call it the crested copepod. This is a chubby creature as far as copepods go, which is why it is number one on the Cassin's auklet's menu. The locally abundant crested copepod might be the reason for the millions of Cassin's auklets nesting on islands on the edge of the continental shelf. After the breeding season comes to a close, the Cassin's auklet migrates to the edge of the continental shelf off California. There are close to three million Cassin's auklets on the Jade Coast but they are largely unknown to most people.

One of the most unusual seabirds on the Jade Coast is the ancient murrelet. One place they inhabit is Limestone Island, tucked away in the sheltered east coast of the Queen Charlotte Islands. This tiny seabird nests in underground burrows they dig among the roots of ancient rainforests along the Jade Coast. Unlike other seabirds that raise their young to a good size before leaving for the sea, the ancient murrelet chicks leave their burrows to follow the parents to sea one or two days after hatching. Starting near midnight, the tiny chicks scamper across the moss-covered forest floor to the sea, drawn by the calling of their parents and an inherent attraction to light. By daylight, they have swum far out to sea.[22]

Tony Gaston from the Canadian Wildlife Service has researched the ancient murrelet on Limestone Island. The threat of oil drilling in nearby Hecate Strait meant that more information was needed on the birds' life history for conservation to be effective. Tony and a group of keen individuals from the Queen Charlottes established the Laskeek Bay Conservation Society to understand the seabirds and the ecology of the region. A rustic camp was built and, for over a decade, volunteers and a few paid staff have maintained the station. Visitors are welcomed to the island by prior appointment at the Laskeek Bay Conservation Society's office in Queen Charlotte City. A tour by day provides visitors with an orientation to the island, its work and its inhabitants, but the real excitement comes at night.

A Boat Trip from the Deep and across the Shelf

Hecate Strait separates the Queen Charlotte Islands from the mainland of British Columbia. At places the sea is not more than 50 meters (162 feet) deep and the Strait is legendary for its rough seas. One way to tell how far your boat is from land (and to relieve seasickness) is to observe the birds. In the deep ocean, where the water is over two and a half kilometers (1.5 miles) deep, you might spot the Buller's Shearwater. Land is a long way off. If the sooty shearwater, fork-tailed storm-petrel, Cassin's auklet and California gull are seen, the boat must be passing over the slope of the continental shelf.

Along the continental shelf, the rich plankton meadows provide food for the humpback whale and the abundant herring supply food for the fleet of Dall's porpoise. Their sloppy table manners attract flocks of fork-tailed storm-petrels. The Thayer's gull, glaucous-winged gull, Sabine's gull, and Cassin's auklet inhabit waters on the shelf of about 45 to 200 meters (150 to 650 feet) deep. As land comes into view, so do Pacific loons, double-crested cormorants, white-winged scoter, with more California gulls and a few Cassin's auklets, and as the swell subsides, pigeon guillemots become numerous.

My tour group entered the island via a pirate cove on the western shore. Darkness obscured the entrance while we strained to see the Limestone crew's boat tendered to a sea line in the middle of the bay. We glided past, leaving a stream of bioluminescent plankton swirling in the wake. Once ashore, we followed like a troop of Druids into the forest. I find the forest at night especially intriguing because the nocturnal animals are about. A saw-whet owl chirped in the forest. A blue grouse hooted in the distance even though darkness had fallen an hour earlier. We trod up and down the trail until we reached the far beach where we met biologist Joanna Smith whose job was to band nestling murrelets and inform the public of the aims of the research. I found a comfortable place to wait for the return of the murrelets. Far out at sea, a common murre laughed and a humpback whale blew. The white of the surf gleamed along the rocky shores.

Some time about midnight the first murrelet arrived in the forest with a whir of wings. It slipped into the forest to chirp in the trees up the slope behind us. Then a few more arrived, and before too long the forest was alive with chirps, squeals, whirs and thumps of murrelets. They were in the trees, on the ground and on the ocean, uttering calls to their chicks to run for the sea. That evening, a few chicks made the run on large legs for the relative safety of the ocean. Across logs, around boulders and tumbling down gullies they came. The low fences built by the Laskeek Bay Conservation Society funneled the chicks toward us. I caught one in my hands and scurried off to meet up with Joanna. She weighed, measured, banded and released the tiny chick near the beach in about five minutes. It chirped as it scurried to the water where its parent was waiting.

I have witnessed the running of the murrelets many times and it never fails to astound me that such a small chick can survive the rigors of ocean life within two days of hatching. Tony has tracked these mites and found them several kilometers at sea by morning. I am also impressed by the dedication, passion and enthusiasm of the crews that conduct the work. They sleep during the day and work at night for several weeks until the season ends. The memories will stay with them for the rest of their lives.

Two other species of shorebird that frequent the open ocean are the Red-necked Phalarope and the Red Phalarope. Both are dainty shorebirds that migrate along the Pacific Coast in flocks of hundreds to thousands. They settle on the sea where there are concentrations of plankton and swim in a characteristic twirling motion, picking up food particles swirling around them. Phalaropes are masterful migrants. Red-necked Phalaropes will spend the winter off Peru, and Red Phalaropes off Australia.

FISH PREDATORS

The Jade Coast is home to many species of fish-eating birds. The black-footed albatross leaves its nestling in the Hawaiian Islands to cross the Pacific in search of food along the Jade Coast. The sooty shearwater circumnavigates the Pacific

Death of the Albatross

The American Bird Conservancy has been pushing for a change in the longline fishery because of its toll on seabirds. The Conservancy estimates that an average of 20,000 seabirds drown annually in the Alaska longline fishery. The problem arises when the birds snatch baited hooks on longlines tailing behind fishing vessels. The mortality falls especially hard on the slow-reproducing albatross. From 1993 to 1999, over 2,400 black-footed albatrosses were killed in Alaska. The problem is widespread in the world's oceans.

Seabird Islands

The Pacific Ocean is home to a plethora of seabirds. The breeding species include puffins, auklets, murres, murrelets, gulls, fulmars, petrels, and cormorants. Shearwaters and albatrosses breed in the southern Pacific Ocean and visit the north Pacific during the southern winter. Seabirds spend all but a brief few months during the breeding season at sea and when they come ashore, they often seek out islands devoid of most land predators. However, 98 percent of the islands are left unused, not because they harbor predators but because they are in the wrong place. For a seabird, breeding requires immense amounts of food. In British Columbia, seabirds prefer islands in cold, saline water and relatively lower rainfall[23] because plankton and fish are abundant in these conditions.

from its breeding grounds off New Zealand to spend the boreal summer along the Jade Coast. The California gull breeds in colonies on the Canadian prairies and in the American Midwest and migrates to the Jade Coast for the winter. Many seabirds that breed along the Pacific Coast exploit the spring abundance of food near their colonies and join migrant seabirds from around the world to take advantage of the abundance of food at upwelling areas and tidally active channels. The large-bodied seabirds such as the rhinoceros auklet, tufted puffin, common murre and California gull are essentially fish-eaters while the moderate-sized ancient murrelet crosses over with a diet of both fish and euphausiids.

Inshore waters are the home of the pelagic, double-crested and Brandt's cormorant. Brandt's cormorants tend to be the more southerly of the three cormorant species, double-crested cormorants occupy the southern and mid-coast, and the pelagic cormorant is the more northerly species. The three species also exploit their fish prey in different ways. Brandt's cormorants form into flocks in the hundreds to pursue schooling sandlance and herring in deep water. The double-crested cormorants fish alone and in small flocks on shiner perch, sculpins and other fish in shallow muddy areas. The pelagic cormorant usually feeds alone on gunnels and other small fish that live along rocky shores.

A ubiquitous seabird on the Jade Coast is the pigeon guillemot. During the breeding season, its black plumage and white patches on the wings make it a conspicuous denizen in most parts of the coast. It eats mostly small fish and is eaten by eagles, falcons, octopus and killer whales.

Whales

Abundant as the whales may be in the vicinity of Nootka, they bear no comparison to the numbers seen on the Northern part of the coast: Indeed the generality of these huge marine mammals delight the frozen climates.
– John Meares, 1790

It was the dead of summer, and the morning air was cloaked in an Alaskan fog. Heavy dew that coated our boat as she lay at anchor in a small cove for the night dropped from the rigging to splash on the deck. The gray-green sea lapped against the hull as the *Island Roamer* slid through the fog. Onboard, we were sipping coffee and watching the green radar screen reveal distant islands as we slipped out to sea. I could hear the ocean swell breaking into a deep growl on a distant headland somewhere out in the fog. Suddenly, the mood changed as the rising sun turned the sullen gray fog into dazzling gold. The white hull gleamed, drops of dew quivered in the cool air and suddenly a humpback whale rolled past the port side. Randy stopped the engine and from all around us, we could hear the deep guttural inhaling of whales. We were surrounded by a pod of what sounded like a dozen or more humpback whales feeding on herring. We strained to see them, but the whales were just out of sight in the golden mist. We inched forward for a few minutes, and the mist began to dissipate under a clean, blue sky. Not more than 50 meters (163 feet) away the whales were puffing and blowing in preparation for a dive that would take them below for several minutes. A shiver ran up my spine. It was such a pleasure to witness these huge animals going about their activities so unconcerned about our presence that we stayed for over an hour.

In 1976, I saw my first humpback whale, not in the cool waters of the Jade Coast but from Maui in the Hawaiian Islands. Amidst the aroma of coconut sunscreen, cries of children playing in the surf, and warm tropical breezes, I spotted a blow from a humpback whale a few kilometers off shore. The whales leave Alaskan feeding grounds in autumn and begin to arrive in Hawaii in late

Humpback whales in Frederick Sound, Alaska cooperate to catch herring. The whales begin their descent into a school of herring milling at the water surface. From below, a whale swims in a circle exhaling bursts of bubbles. The death ring of bubbles rising through the water frightens the herring into a tight school near the surface where several whales erupt with mouths full of herring.

October. The trip takes an estimated forty days or more. About 4000 humpbacks spend the winter in Hawaii, where females give birth to their calves. They depart from April to early June.

Along some of the shores of southeast Alaska, the humpback whale exhibits a spectacular feeding behavior.[24] About 100 humpbacks assemble in Frederick Sound each summer to gorge on schools of herring and krill. The herring could evade the slow-moving humpbacks under normal circumstances but the whales have developed a well-choreographed trick to keep herring from escaping. When disturbed, schools of herring dive into deep water to evade predators such as whales, salmon and dogfish. To foil these attempts, the humpbacks dive to about

20 meters (65 feet) below the surface. From below the school of fish, one whale emits a ring of air bubbles through its blowhole in a 5 to 10 meter (16 to 33 feet) wide circle. The herring respond to the rising ring of bubbles by swimming into a tight ball. The rising bubbles move the frightened ball slowly upward toward the surface of the water. The humpbacks use their exceptionally long pectoral fins to direct the herring. Moments after the bubbles surface, a phalanx of whales with huge mouths agape erupt from below, scooping thousands of herring into their cavernous mouths in one gulp. This leviathan ballet must be finely played to be effective; any deeper than 20 meters (65 feet), the bubbles disintegrate into small bubbles and the herring escape.

Sighting whales is often the highlight of a visit to the sea, and among the top-billing species is the killer whale, or orca. Much has been learned about the diet, distribution and vocalizations of killer whales. Two distinct groups of killer whales are frequently seen in the north Pacific. One group resides in distinct regions of the coast where they eat salmon moving toward spawning rivers. These are known as "resident" killer whales, and pods typically contain between fifteen and sixty individuals. In 2002 there were seventy-nine residents in southern British Columbia and Washington, 200 in northern British Columbia, and about 500 in southeast Alaska. A second group of whales is elusive, eating mostly seals, sea lions and porpoises, and they travel alone or in small, quiet groups. These "transients" steal quickly through the islands. There were about 100 transients in California and 220 in Washington, British Columbia and Alaska. Both resident and transient whales have distinctively shaped dorsal fins and markings, suggesting genetic differences.[25] The third group of about 250 whales found mostly far from land and referred to as "offshores." They travel in large groups but make long, erratic dives similar to transients. The shape of their dorsal fins is

Whale Watching

One of the most popular places to see orcas or killer whales is Limekiln State Park on the southern shore of San Juan Island, Washington. From July through September killer whales intercept the immense schools of salmon approaching the Fraser River here.

The best time to see gray whales is during spring migration, when they are near shore. The peak passage of whales without calves precedes the mother/calf migration by many weeks. As a result, migrating whales can be seen from California to Alaska in March and April. The peak passage of females without calves is late February in California, mid-March in Oregon and Washington, and April in British Columbia. Mothers and calves follow about six weeks later. Ecola viewpoint and Neahkahnie Mountain are favorites among whale-watching aficionados in Oregon, Tofino is a favorite in British Columbia, and Seward and Kodiak are good sites in Alaska. Choose a calm day and bring binoculars.

Orcas or killer whales roam the entire Jade Coast. In late summer, many orcas assemble in Johnstone Strait, British Columbia and in Haro Strait near San Juan Island, Washington to hunt salmon returning to coastal rivers to spawn.

intermediate between the rounded form of the residents and the more pointed shape of transients. The white "saddle patch" on their backs does not have any intruding black markings typical of residents, and their bodies are generally smaller than the resident or transient whales. The current theory is that offshore whales are smaller in size because they live in the less productive waters beyond the continental shelf, a feature shared by other offshore species of whales.[25]

The largest-toothed whale on Earth is the sperm whale – males reach 18 meters (60 feet) in length, and females reach about 12 meters (40 feet). The sperm whale has the largest brain on Earth, the greatest geographical separation between the sexes, dives deeper than any other mammal, and has one of the most caring societies among marine mammals.

In many ways, the social behavior of sperm whales is similar to that of elephants in that both species remain in groups led by matriarchs in which aunts care for offspring while mothers are away.[26] Next to the killer whale, the sperm whale has the widest distribution of marine mammals in the world. Females and young are generally restricted to tropical waters and seldom venture north of about 42 degrees north, but males range into temperate seas on a regular basis.

Sperm whales frequent continental shelves, large islands and offshore banks where upwelling creates rich feeding grounds. Males compete for opportunities to breed; consequently younger and smaller bulls linger in the north to grow in size whereas the mature bulls are farther south with females.[26] A mainstay of their diet is squid, which they hunt by diving deep into the abyss. Diving sperm whales typically reach about 400 meters (1300 feet) underwater during a forty-minute dive followed by about eight minutes of breathing at the surface. Some individuals have been recorded at a depth of 3195 meters (10,482 feet). Sperm whales eat mostly small squid but occasionally eat giant squid. Whale stomachs off Vancouver Island contained squid, ragfish and rockfish.

Other Fish Predators

The northern elephant seal is also a squid eater, diving to depths of 350 to 600 meters (1140 to 1950 feet) to pursue its prey, where it remains submerged for about twenty-five minutes. Elephant seals migrate north from breeding islands in northern Mexico and southern California to feed along the Jade Coast. These journeys can cover about 20,000 kilometers (12,500 miles) in a year. Elephant seals on the Jade Coast were hunted nearly to extinction in the nineteenth century but have since made a remarkable recovery. We now see them occasionally along the northern shores, where they look deceivingly similar to barely floating waterlogged logs.

It is also becoming increasingly common to see white-sided dolphins along the Jade Coast. They are very playful around boats, and I have watched them ride the wake of a boat within reach of outstretched arms. Dolphins feed largely on schooling fish such as herring by crippling the clumsy and slow fish

Tales of Destruction

Herman Melville's tale of the fury of a sperm whale, Moby Dick, was a fictionalized version of a true story of a sperm whale attacking a whaling boat in 1820. There had been numerous accounts of whaling boats and ships capsizing following collisions with sperm whales, but it was the attack on the whaleship *Essex* in the Pacific that captured Melville's imagination. The first mate and cabin boy wrote accounts of the attack in which a large bull sperm whale hit the bow of the *Essex* with its head with such force as to knock the crew off their feet. Stunned by the collision, the great whale surfaced and slowly began to recover. The crew watched in horror as the whale snapped its jaws, thrashed the water with its tail and then turned to face the bow. With head lifted out of the water, the whale charged the ship, crashing into the bow just below the anchor. Seawater surged into the ship and it began to sink. The whale swam off, leaving the crew in small whaling boats thousands of miles out to sea.[27]

Human Predators

The sea life along the Pacific Coast has undergone significant change in the past few centuries. We lost the sea cow, and the sea otter and several whales have been greatly decimated.

The whaling grounds for the sperm whale was 370 kilometers (230 miles) west of Vancouver Island where herds of fifty to 150 animals were encountered from spring to autumn. Few are seen today.

Tens of thousands of sperm whales were killed in the North Pacific by the whaling industry, especially between 1825 and 1845. American whalers sailing out of New England killed an estimated 225,000 sperm whales between 1804 and 1876. In 1837, the whalers' best year in the nineteenth century, they caught 6,767 sperm whales. Total catches listed by whaling stations from 1910 to 1976 totaled over 250,000 sperm whales. Sperm whales were killed in two large-scale hunts: one between the eighteenth and early twentieth centuries, when whalers used rowing boats and hand-thrown harpoons, and a second between 1946 and 1978 when whalers in diesel-powered boats with deck-mounted harpoons took hundreds of animals.

At its peak in 1964 modern whaling killed 29,255 sperm whales. Today there are about two million sperm whales roaming the sea. We are only now starting to get an insight of what these changes might bring as abundant species are replaced by less common species.[28] Ecologists better understand now what happens when species are lost from their food webs. The rules guiding the competition and predation change. Species that were once rare now flourish as they find a sudden abundance of food and scarcity of predators.

during high-speed lunges. (In the case of herring, staying in school really pays off!) Watching a pod of hundreds of dolphins frothing the water as they gobble up herring that stray from the school, and then darting off to a newfound school, is dizzying.

Another playful animal, and the most abundant marine mammal in the north Pacific, is the Dall's porpoise. It is at home in straits, sounds and channels, where the water depth is about 20 meters (65 feet), and over the continental shelf and open ocean, where the water depth is 2,500 meters (8,125 feet) is the. It hunts mostly deep-dwelling fish and squid. A spray of water rooster-tailing behind the dorsal fin is a characteristic of the Dall's porpoise.

Other fish predators along the Jade Coast include the Minke whale and the harbor porpoise. The Minke whale is a small baleen whale that eats sardines, anchovies, herring and copepods, and the harbor porpoise eats herring and other small fish. Harbor porpoises are retiring animals that never ride waves set up by boats.

LIFE AT DAVY JONES' LOCKER

Lying along the ocean floor over 165 meters (536 feet) from the surface of Hecate Strait is a remarkable sponge reef that covers about 700 square kilometers (260 square miles) of the seabed. While the size of the reef is remarkable, what most intrigues the scientists who discovered it is the age of the sponges. The same species were present on Earth 65 million years ago.[29]

Even deeper in the ocean than the sponges lies a recently discovered food web. In the ocean's abyss live creatures that depend on the volcanism of the earth for their livelihood. Lying over 1.5 kilometers (1.0 mile) below the surface of the ocean, the sea vents or "black smokers" emit hot water with a temperature of 350 degrees Celsius (662 degrees Fahrenheit) and seem an unlikely place to find any living creature, but they are alive with Pandora worms, meter (39 inch) -long tubeworms, octopi, snails, limpets and rat-tailed fish. Over 200 species of animals have been found here.

The basis of food webs of most living creatures on Earth is photosynthesis, but at the bottom of the ocean, bacteria thriving in the warm water and hydrogen-sulphide bubbling from the Earth provide food for a chain of other creatures. But the story is even more intriguing. The giant tubeworms and the bacteria have worked out a unique partnership. The tubeworm has long since discarded its mouth and digestive system in favor of an organ packed with bacteria – a "trophosome." The tubeworm absorbs carbon dioxide and oxygen from the seawater and hydrogen-sulphide from the sea vent. The hydrogen-sulphide is then shipped to the trophosome where the bacteria combine the oxygen into energy and produce a steady supply of sugars, fats and amino acids for the worms. Presumably the other creatures eat the worms and one another.

The great westerly winds that drive the north Pacific ocean ecosystem eventually collide with the North American continent, where the Pacific releases its immense energy in waves that pound the rocky shores of the Jade Coast. Creatures that live in this high-energy zone are very different from those of the open ocean, and they are the subjects of the next chapter.

Rocky shores are often festooned with animals and plants that anchor to the solid rock. Cabbage Island, British Columbia.

CHAPTER 4

Rocky Shores

... each November great waves awake and are drawn
Like smoking mountain bright from the west
And come and cover the cliff with white violent cleanness ...
Like the steep necks of a herd of horses
Lined on a river margin, athirst in summer, the mountain ridges
Pitch to the sea, the lean granite-boned heads
Plunge nostril under ...
– Robinson Jeffers, *Not Man Apart*

Brooks Peninsula protrudes from Vancouver Island like a large thumb pointing to the southwest. Tucked behind the Brooks lies perilous Checleset Bay where scores of small islands, rocks and reefs keep mariners on their toes. The air is unbelievably fresh here, and the pounding sea is relentless. To survive this battle zone, animals and plants on rocky headlands anchor, shield, bend or hide from the fury.

Despite these capricious conditions, rocky shores are festooned with delicate-looking seaweeds. The tangled beds of glistening pink, golden-brown, green, and shimmering iridescent seaweeds are the source of food for a host of snails, chitons (pronounced "*kite-on*") and limpets whose lives are tied to those of seabirds, fish and marine mammals. In the subtidal reaches of the rocky shore dwells the greatest diversity of rockfish in the world, with names picked from an artist's palette: There are vermilion, copper, dusky, brown rockfish, yellowtail and yelloweye, and blue, black, greenstripe and redstripe rockfish. The rocky shore is also home to the world's largest octopus, chiton, barnacle, and sea slug, and the heaviest starfish. There are 68 species of seastars, 111 sea slugs, and over 400 amphipods. And some of the relationships between plants, animals and their environment on the rocky shores along the Pacific Coast have become classic examples in teachings of ecology.[1]

I visited Checleset Bay in the 1980s to tally seabirds and collect a few eggs for contaminant residues. We had been working along treacherous rocky shores in inflatable boats. These small boats are very seaworthy and could enter shallow waters that larger boats could not. We had stopped to rest on a small island in late afternoon. The angle of the evening sun's rays created long blue shadows on the beach. Not far away were the remains of a garbage heap, or midden, of a long abandoned fishing camp of the Nuu-chah-nulth people, who today live mostly in nearby villages. Middens such as these are numerous along the coast wherever food was plentiful. Waves and wind had exposed years of discarded clamshells. I found myself staring at the midden as if I had come upon a long out-of-print book. I was imagining how each layer of discarded shells represented the lives of people long ago. At what point among the layers of shells, I pondered, did the first native people encounter Europeans?

In the evening light, my eye caught upon a small sea otter jawbone protruding from the shells. Checleset Bay was the centre of a thriving but short-lived trade in sea otters between the Nuu-chah-nulth, the Europeans and the Chinese in the nineteenth and twentieth centuries. I imagined that the jawbone had lain there for two centuries, since Maquinna, chief of the Nuu-chah-nulth, looked out to sea to the approaching HMS *Discovery* and *Resolution* under the command of James Cook. In the midden lay a story of the demise of the sea otter and then it stopped abruptly when the Nuu-chah-nulth left the area. Fortunately, there is an epilogue to the sea otter story.

The following day we set out for a remote and surf-swept island. The sun was bright and the westerly wind whipped waves into a froth. The air on days like this is so fresh that green sea and forest stand out in sharp contrast against the cobalt blue sky. We brought our boats into the lee of the small island and tossed our gear ashore. The wind whistled past my ears and the pungent odor of seaweed filled my nostrils. Not far offshore in the rolling surf we caught a glimpse of a sea otter surfacing and diving. We watched for a few minutes before it disappeared around a bend in the island. This was the farthest point south I would see sea otters for over two decades.

In 2002, I joined a group of park wardens in Pacific Rim National Park to explore the Broken Islands in Barkley Sound, nearly 200 kilometers (125 miles) south of Checleset Bay. I was considering establishing a research program in the National Park, and we were investigating possible study sites. There had been numerous reports of sea otters farther north and a few from Barkley Sound.

Otters seem to seek out the outermost islands that take the brunt of the Pacific swell. The most westerly islands of the Broken Islands met that description. We began by tallying gulls, oystercatchers and cormorants on the island. Within minutes, one sea otter appeared in the surf and then a second appeared around a point on the island. About seventy years had lapsed since sea otters swam in those waters. The sighting of these sea otters reminded me how ever-changing ecosystems can be.

The demise of the sea otter from the Pacific Coast is one of the most celebrated cases of ecological disruption. The otters were killed for their pelts beginning in 1741.[2] By 1911, the sea otter, the sprite of the rocky shores, was nearly extinct, leaving its sea urchin prey access to the immense kelp forests along the rocky shores of the Pacific. The trickle-down effect is one of the most oft-cited examples of how human greed caused a major upheaval in an ecosystem.

Before the demise of the sea otter, the Jade Coast lost Steller's sea cow, the only temperate latitude dugong. In 1741, Peter the Great of Russia charged Vitus Bering with the exploration of the north Pacific. Accompanying Bering was naturalist Georg Steller, after whom the Steller's sea cow was named. Within a few years of its discovery, Bering was dead, and the Steller's sea cow, was extinct. The sea cow is in the family *Sirenidae,* presumably a wry taxonomic

Surge Channels

Where the land squeezes into narrow passages, a turn in the tide results in whirlpools, rapids and standing waves. The tremendous volume of water that passes through these narrow passages carries large quantities of plankton. About a decade ago, divers brought to our attention the abundance of life below the surface of the raging waters of Skookumchuck Narrows, near Egmont, north of Vancouver.[3] There, barnacles are tenfold larger than the intertidal species, and coral and gooseneck barnacles typically found in wave-washed surf on the outer coast are present in abundance. Many other passages have been explored and all of them have rich subtidal life. The surge channels are also important sources of larvae for the surrounding waters.

Seaweed beds in some places on the Jade Coast have been clear-cut by sea urchins that were a dietary mainstay of formerly abundant sea otters.

twist of humor in honor of the mythological sea nymph *Sirenia*. Bering stumbled upon the last of the world's sea cows in the remote Kurile Islands of the Aleutian chain, but their remains have been found as far south as California.

Sea cows were massive dugongs that resembled present day manatees. Each animal required massive amounts of seaweeds to sustain its great bulk. Sea cows, like sea otters, might have been inextricably linked in the ecological web of the Pacific rocky shore but we will never know for sure. In contrast, we have learned much about the sea otter's role in rocky shore ecosystems. All that remains today of the sea cow is a patch of skin and a few bones in a museum.

The Nuts and Bolts of Rocky Shores

One foot in sea and one on shore ...– William Shakespeare, *Midsummer Night's Dream*

Plants and animals living in the pounding surf on rocky headlands have evolved some novel means to deal with punishing waves. The sea palm has a strong anchor and flexible stems. But alas, dislodged sea palms become castaways on nearby beaches. Coos Bay, Oregon.

Animals and plants that live on the rocky shores of the Pacific Coast cope with the force of waves, the tearing surge of currents and low-tide periods of hot sun. Colossal winter giants replace the lapping waves of summer. Many plants and animals have adapted to living on wave-washed shores by evolving strong attachments, flexible parts and thick shells. Some animals hide from heavy surf by squeezing into crevices. For the California mussel and the sea palm, the surf is their preferred habitat. The California mussel fine-tunes its anchoring system to the wave action – where surf is strong, it has many more anchoring threads than where surf is weak.[4]

But even the strongest anchors eventually give way to the relentless pounding surf, and waves carrying sand and grit challenge even the most heavily armoured animals. The scouring actions scuff off young animals. Other animals and plants get buried under a shower of sand and stones. Few animals can tolerate relentless scouring, but many species can survive burial for weeks. It is on sand beaches that species are best able to cope with burial. The wash left by waves allows barnacles, mussels and other creatures to live higher on the beach than in calm areas. This can be readily seen on a rocky headland where barnacles on the wave-washed side live higher out of water than on the lee-side.

Currents play a role similar to waves in shaping the distribution of rocky shore creatures. One of the clearest examples of the impact of currents on the distribution of animals is among the barnacles. Barnacles begin their lives as free-swimming larvae, but settle as adults for their rest of their lives. Where they settle is important for growth and reproduction. Sites with low current flows are avoided because less food travels to these places than to sites with good current flow. High current flow prevents settling by sweeping larvae away but, once anchored, barnacles can grow to an immense size.

Crowding can be a problem for many animals on rocky shores. Mussels and gooseneck barnacles feel the squeeze on this rocky shore on the west coast of Vancouver Island.

One of the first things one notices when visiting the rocky shores of the Pacific Coast is the distinct bands of plants and animals on rock surfaces. Near the top of the tide are bands of barnacles and rockweed, followed a little further down by mussels. Near the bottom is a profuse layer of kelp and other seaweeds. Three important reasons for this pattern are the time spent out of water, competition from other organisms and the presence of predators. The upper limit for plants and animals is largely established by desiccation while the lower

Succession in the Sea

As boat owners know, a clean hull requires regular attention to remove the plants and animals seeking a new home. Within a few days of sitting in the water, the hull takes on a slimy feel and several weeks later it will be home to a flourishing assortment of seaweeds, barnacles and mussels. The ocean teams with the swimming stages of many animals familiar to us on the shore – and all of them are trying to find a space to settle down.

Ecologists refer to the order in which plants and animals settle on bare rock and are replaced as "succession." Four stages are clearly recognizable. The first stage involves opportunistic filamentous algae that cling to the bare surface. These are usually the stringy red and green algae. Soon coralline algae shade out and replace these algae. Third are the barnacles that undercut the algae, clearing the way for the fourth stage, during which dominant mussels crowd out algae and barnacles.

limits are set by predation and competition for space and food from other organisms.

Any plant or animal that spends its life attached to a rocky shore of the Pacific Coast must be able to tolerate periods of being submerged when the tide covers the beach. The timing of submergence plays a critical role in the distribution of intertidal organisms. Along much of the Pacific Coast, there are two high and two low tides in about a 25-hour period. Organisms living near the point of the highest tide will be covered by water about once each month, whereas organisms living near the lowest tide will be uncovered about once each month. A gradation of submergence and emergence lies between these two points, and where a plant or animal resides along this gradient will depend on its particular tolerances to air and seawater. This feature is so striking that it has drawn a great deal of attention from marine ecologists.

Space is often in short supply on rocky shores, and competition to settle is fierce. Peaceful-looking barnacles are often locked in an epic struggle for space. Smaller species of barnacle such as *Chthamalus dalli* are uplifted, crushed and overgrown by the larger *Balanus glandula*. In an experiment in which the bullying barnacle was eliminated, *Chthalamus* began to settle in the traditional territory of *Balanus*. However, it is not only barnacles that compete for space.[5] A three-way struggle for a foothold also exists between mussels, barnacles and the sea palm,[6] and limpets compete by bulldozing barnacles from rocks.

Predators such as starfish, whelks and birds are also important in shaping where intertidal plants and animals reside on rocky shores. More on their role follows later in this chapter.

Rocky Shore Food Webs

Together the plankton, seaweed and detritus are the basis of the food chain for all the mouths on the rocky shore.[7] Phytoplankton is eaten by zooplankton, and together they are eaten by many of the familiar filter feeding animals, such as mussels and barnacles. The predators of mussels and barnacles include diving sea ducks, marine snails, and starfish, and they are prey of gulls and eagles. Seaweeds such as kelps and rockweeds are eaten by grazers such as sea urchins, limpets and chitons, which are eaten by swimming predators such as rockfish and octopi, diving predators such as diving ducks and otters, and beach predators such as oystercatchers, crows and mink. The detritus consumers are animals such as the sea cucumber and shore crab.

THE PRODUCERS: PLANKTON AND SEAWEED

Plankton Meadows
The ecology of the plankton meadows described in the previous chapter is so important along the shore that it is worth a brief summary here. The spring freshet, burdened with sediments washing from the land and the upwelling of nutrients from the ocean depths, enriches the coastal zone from California to Alaska. The lengthening days of spring trigger the rebirth of plankton meadows, creating a green ribbon of plankton along the Pacific Coast. One of the richest plankton zones lies in the waters surrounding the rocky shores of Puget Sound and the Strait of Georgia.

Like most plants, phytoplankton use energy from the sun to produce starch and sugars. Nutrients are absorbed from the surrounding seawater. Within the plankton meadows are tiny animals, known as zooplankton, which live on phytoplankton or prey on one another. These tiny animals include a host of species that are familiar to us in their adult stages, including crabs, sea cucumbers, starfish, clams and some species of fish, as well as species that spend their entire life as zooplankton. Phytoplankton are far more numerous than marine algae restricted to the fringe of rocky shores. However, the same nutrients and sunlight that trigger the growth of phytoplankton also fuel the growth of marine algae.

Seaweed Gardens

There are four kinds of marine algae, also known as seaweeds, and most are distinguishable by pigmentation. Blue-green algae form a scummy growth on wet soil and in shallow water. Green algae, such as sea lettuce, are usually bright green and live high on the beach. Brown algae include the kelps and predominate among algae on rocky beaches. Red algae are predominantly red to almost black in color and inhabit deeper water. The pigmentation of seaweeds is a response to available light for photosynthesis. Deep-water species absorb the longer wavelengths of

The more than 500 species of marine algae along the Jade Coast are food for grazing animals and shelter for others. A rocky shore in Kyuquot Sound, British Columbia, festooned with algae provides an undersea garden for small animals.

Kelp Forests

Kelp forests are a conspicuous feature of the Jade Coast rocky shoreline. In the protected waters, the bull kelp predominates, and along most of the exposed outer coast, bull kelp and sugar wrack are common. Within their fronds swaying in the ocean currents live crabs, snails, fish and mammals. Kelps are held in place by a holdfast that resembles a leathery root. Its function is simply to anchor the plant in place, but within its tangled mat live shrimps, worms and other invertebrates. Kelp forests provide shelter for a variety of fish and invertebrates.

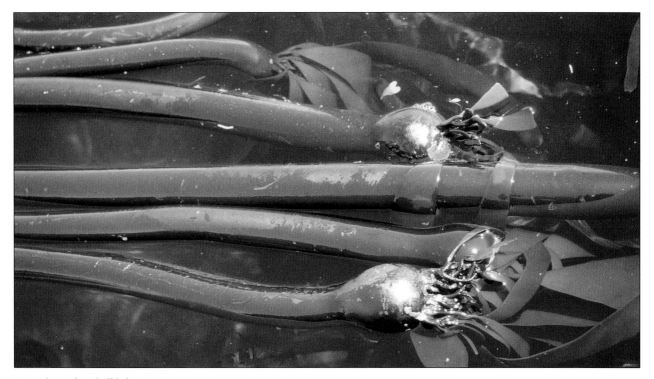

From the surface, bull kelp appears to be a jumble of seaweed, but underwater it forms into a graceful floating forest for fish and marine invertebrates along the shores of the Jade Coast.

light, such as the green and blue spectrum, which penetrate farthest in water. Shallow dwelling species absorb shorter wavelengths in the red spectrum. Algae seldom exceed 2 meters (80 inches) in length in the intertidal region of the beach, but some deep-water species grow over 25 meters (80 feet) long.

Seaweeds are some of the most distinctive organisms on rocky shores. Near the top of the rocky beach will be a band of olive-colored rockweeds also known as *fucus,* pronounced "*few-kus.*" Usually nearby is a limp-looking leafy alga called *Porphyra.* Clinging to rocks in tidal pools and protected shores lives Dead Man's Fingers, as well as some of our most beautiful seaweeds – the coralline seaweeds. The calcium carbonate cell walls that resemble white coral when dried are thought to serve as a deterrent to grazing urchins and snails.

Seaweed reaches its greatest species diversity on the lower region of the beach. Many species of seaweed occur here, including the abundant sugar wrack, the lacy-looking feather boa, the iridescent *Mazaella cordata,* the wing kelp, and the 20-meter (65-foot) bull kelp. The latter form huge beds along the shore and supports a community of life among its fronds. A remarkable species of seaweed is the surf-loving sea palm, which clings to headlands lashed by the sea. The largest marine alga is the giant kelp (*Macrocystis*) whose daily growth rate equals or exceeds that of tropical bamboos.[8]

Marine algae are simple plants with little differentiation in their structure. The seawater brings nutrients to the entire plant and provides support so that the plant can reach into the sunlight. Hence, many seaweeds have not evolved the specialized leaves and stems of land-dwelling plants to transport nutrients and wastes. Many types of seaweed have prodigious growth. One has only to wade through the slippery algal-covered rocks at low tide to recognize the magnitude of growth that takes place along these shores.

The Detritus

> *Ever drifting, drifting, drifting,*
> *On the shifting*
> *Currents of the restless main,*
> *Till in the sheltered coves, and reaches*
> *Of sandy beaches,*
> *All have found repose again.*
> – Henry Wadsworth Longfellow, "Seaweed"

Detritus consists largely of dead particles of seaweeds that result when invertebrates such as snails, limpets and chitons graze, and from the destructive force of storms. About 10 percent of the seaweed produced along the shore becomes detritus. Another 35 to 40 percent comes from carbohydrate molecules that are released during photosynthesis rather than going into plant growth. This material is an important early step in the food web since it provides food to many invertebrates. A smaller source of detritus is the remains of victims killed by predators. Dead animals enter the detrital food web via scavengers. The detrital food web is immense and largely invisible to the untrained eye. It is created by the chemical action of marine bacteria that make the detritus digestible

The bay mussel forms into distinctive tightly packed bands of animals near the top of the beach of many rocky shores where the salinity of the water is diluted by freshwater.

69

by other animals, and by the consumption of the detritus by amphipods and filter feeders.

Filter Feeders

Two conspicuous animals on rocky shores are the blue and California mussels. They crowd along the mid-tide level of rocky shores, edging out other species. The California mussel is the monster of mussels, reaching up to 20 centimeters (8 inches) in length. Often nearby are the goose-necked barnacles. Both of these open-coast dwellers are replaced in calm waters behind islands and in fjords by the smaller blue mussel.[9]

Mussels are filter feeders that eat from the vast plankton meadows bathing the rocky shores of the Pacific Coast. Food is all around them, so mussels have taken up a sedentary life style in which feeding requires only opening the shells and filtering the seawater. Plankton suspended in the water are drawn in across the gills between the partly opened shells. As the tide drops, mussels tightly close their shells to preserve precious moisture.

Forming a white band on the rocks above the mussels are many species of the volcano-shaped acorn barnacles. These filter feeders wave tiny feathery appendages known as cirri through the water to snare microscopic plankton, which are then brought to the mouth. Unlike the grazers that are scattered here and there along rocky shores, filter feeders cram together in huge numbers for safety. They begin life as part of the planktonic soup, during which time most is eaten by other animals, including adult filter feeders. Later, if they survive to become sessile adults on rocks, they will have to contend with predatory starfish and birds.

Grazers

Many grazers emerge from their low-tide resting places when seawater splashes them awake to cut a swath through algae on rocks, shells and debris. More often than not, the absence of algae on intertidal rocks is a result of the hordes of grazing snails, limpets and chitons that emerge to feed during high tides. Others set about to devour discarded bits of seaweed and diatoms on the rocks.

The number of species of grazers is immense and includes amphipods, snails, chitons, urchins, and abalones, among others. These animals are important prey for a horde of predators. Surprisingly, the often numerous grazers on rocky shores are supported by only about 10 percent of seaweed plant production; the remaining 90 percent of the seaweeds' production is in the form of carbohydrates, which are dissolved in seawater while the plant is growing or broken down into detritus.

The dominant grazers of the lower rocky shore are the sea urchins. They can wreak havoc on kelp forests by denuding the rocky shores much the same way that fires can influence the succession of terrestrial plant communities.[10] Two species that predominate are the red sea urchin and the purple sea urchin. The former species prefers the calm, sheltered regions of the coast whereas the latter species frequents the wave-torn outer shore. Urchins pass bits of seaweed to the mouth with the help of tube feet.

Another grazing invertebrate is the exquisite northern abalone, which inhabits the subtidal regions along with the urchins. Higher on the shore, several small grazers keep the rocks bare of algae. The limpets are snails with rounded shells that come to a point resembling a hat. The most abundant species include the fingered limpet and shield limpet. The black turban is also part of the team of grazers.

Clinging to rocks are several species of chitons that range from the beautiful, brightly colored lined chiton to the hairy and mossy chiton. The enormous gumboot chiton sometimes exceeds 20 centimetres (8 inches) in length – slightly below the requirement for a B horror film. At the top of the beach, where the highest tides dampen the rocks for brief spells, live the periwinkles. So numerous are these tiny slate-gray snails that in places they form dense clusters in sheltered crevices.

Tide Pools

Tidal pools allow rocky shore creatures to remain active even when the tide leaves other regions high and dry. Barnacles wave their feathery cirri, mussels puff and blow, and around the rim of the rock are several filter feeders not often seen out of water. Among these are several sponges, such as the bright red *Ophlitaspongia pennata*. Lying in wait for any small animal to stumble into their flower-like mouths are the anemones. The sponge is eaten by a nudibranch that is as red as its sponge diet. Appearing like a feathery red flower at the bottom of pools are the feeding tentacles of the burrowing sea cucumber, which extract detritus and plankton from the water. The hermit crab is often numerous and conspicuous in tide pools where it scavenges and eats detritus. Flitting hither and yon is the dappled tide pool sculpin, which scavenges from dead animals and snaps up small crustaceans and worms.[11]

SCAVENGERS AND DETRITUS EATERS
If a sea cucumber can be thought of as beautiful, then my vote is cast in favor of *Cucumaria miniata*. It has brightly colored feathery tentacles on which

Limpet Escape Response

Starfish are major predators in the intertidal region occupied by limpets. Species of limpet that regularly encounter starfish "run" from the predators. Others pull a slippery mantle over their shell that acts as a deterrent. As you might expect, the fingered limpet that lives high on the beach and seldom encounters starfish do not respond to experimentally introduced starfish. But then neither did the suitably named dunce cap limpet that inhabits the lower beaches inhabited by many starfish.[12]

detritus settles and is drawn into the mouth. This species is literally a gutless wonder. If forced to take a defensive stand, it withdraws into its rocky burrow, and if extracted, it can eviscerate its guts as a last resort.

Many rocky shore creatures that scavenge dead plants or animals are also predators. The green shore crab prefers calm water, and the purple shore crab favors exposed shores. Both species eat sea lettuce but they will also scavenge meat when it is available. The porcelain crab is sometimes found in rocky areas, but the most pugnacious and outgoing species is the red rock crab. It challenges any takers with a threatening set of pincers. The red rock crab is a fierce predator and scavenges dead animals that settle on the sea floor.

Eagles, gulls and crows are both scavengers and predators. Eagles spend most of their foraging time perched atop a lookout post waiting for food to come into sight or watching gulls and other eagles that might have located prey. Gulls are more mobile than eagles, and spend their time riding the wind to and fro along beaches looking for morsels. Crows search among the rocky shores near their nests for crabs, snails, fish and clams.

Stay-at-Home and Wanderlust Periwinkles

The similarity of the outward appearance of the Sitka periwinkle and checkered periwinkle belie a very different life style. Although both presumably graze on the same algae, the checkered periwinkle is better able to hang on in rough surf than its calm-water cousin. Furthermore, the Sitka periwinkle lays its eggs in a gelatinous mass in damp areas of the beach that hatch directly as miniature snails whereas the checkered periwinkle eggs become part of the plankton at sea. As a result, the Sitka periwinkle offspring settle near to home whereas the checkered periwinkle young populate distant shores.[13]

PREDATORS

Predators on the Rocks

The principal predators of rocky shore animals are starfish, snails and birds. Along much of the Jade Coast, the ochre or purple star is the predominant starfish, the dog whelk is a conspicuous predatory snail, and the black oyster-catcher an influential avian predator.

The purple starfish is an active hunter that searches and pursues prey during high tides. Once the prey has been subdued, the stomach is everted out the mouth and around the prey. The most frequently eaten prey of the purple star are the barnacles, but the much larger black leather chiton and California mussel provide most of its food energy.

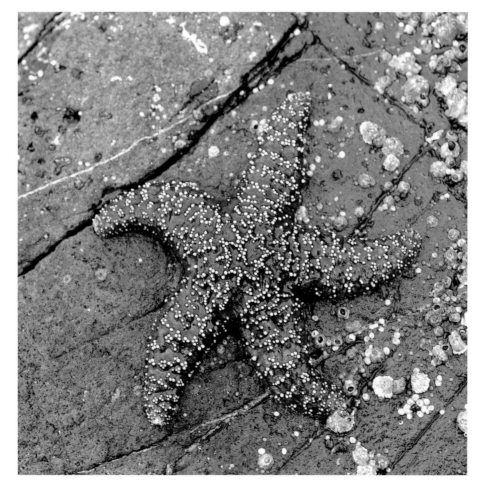

Purple starfish are rapacious predators of mussels and barnacles. They lurk in deep water or hide in crevices during low tides to emerge to eat when the flooding tide covers the rocks.

73

The Standoff between Stars and Mussels

Purple starfish are such effective predators that they can restrict the depth at which mussels live on a beach. When starfish are present, grazing limpets that normally scour rocks of young seaweed fall prey to the starfish. The shortage of limpets allows the red alga *Endocladia muricata* to flourish on the rock surface and provides a home base on which young mussels settle, which then become prey for the starfish. Starfish ravage the mussels' beds during high tides but seek refuge in deeper water, under rocks and in cracks to avoid being eaten by gulls during low tides. This retreat allows mussels to find a foothold high on the beach, although they prefer to live in deeper water.

The whelks are important predators of barnacles, but this one is busy producing a new generation.

The dog whelk is a major predator of barnacles, especially the widespread acorn barnacle *Balanus glandula*. Whelks carve small holes in barnacle shells by the abrasive licking motion of file-like projections on their tongues known as "radula." Eugene Kozloff from the University of Washington thinks that whelks might use a toxin to relax the barnacle shells and thereby gain entry.

The oystercatcher uses its long chisel-shaped beak to lever and chip unsuspecting limpets from rocks. The presence of an oystercatcher limits the number of large limpets, thereby allowing seaweeds and small limpets to flourish. In this fashion, the oystercatcher dictates the number and species of limpets on the beach.[14]

The oystercatcher's life is intimately tied to the movement of tides because all of its food is found in the intertidal region. When the tide ebbs, the oystercatcher enjoys a world full of life on the rocks that is fuelled by the floating beds of phytoplankton and a coastal fringe of seaweeds. When the tide is high, the oystercatcher's kitchen is closed so they snooze, badger one another over nesting borders, and tend their young.

The black oystercatcher is a resident shorebird on the Jade Coast, where it uses it chisel-shaped bill to open shellfish. The presence of oyster-catchers can effect the abundance and size of limpets along rocky shores.

Nesting Oystercatchers

The black oystercatcher nests from the Aleutian Islands to Baja California. Throughout its range, it nests predominantly on rocky shores where it lays two or three eggs in a nest of shell and rock fragments. The young oystercatcher chicks accompany their parent to nearby beaches to be fed on invertebrates. Oystercatchers live for many years and return to the same island to breed each year.

Do oystercatchers catch oysters? There were few oysters on the Jade Coast until the introduction of the Japanese oyster about a century ago, but in one place, oystercatchers have become masters over the molluscs. Many years ago, I was studying the social behavior of crows on a small island off the coast of British Columbia. Japanese oysters had been seeded into a small bay on the south shore of the island, and each morning a pair of oystercatchers had their fill. My curiosity got the better of me, and so each morning while eating breakfast, I noted how the oystercatchers dispatched their oyster quarry. I wanted to know how they removed the immense mollusc from its shell. Would they pry open the two shells or hammer a hole through the shell? It turned out that they hammered. They used their chisel-like bill to chip a small hole in the oyster shell, gaining entry to the muscle holding the shells tightly in place. A few snips and the muscle was severed, the two shells opened, and the oystercatcher dined on the tender meat inside. It had taken only a few decades for these oystercatchers to master the new skill required to open the hard-shelled oyster.[14]

The glaucous-winged gull is a predator of the intertidal zone with a catholic diet. It preys on barnacles, snails, chitons, limpets, mussels, sea urchins, crabs, starfish and fish, among other things. During neap low tides, the gull concentrates on eating barnacles and mussels but on spring low tides it nearly abandons these animals in favor of urchins, chitons, and limpets.[14]

Swimming Predators

The intertidal portion of the rocky shore holds many species of small fish that are important prey for birds, mammals and other fish. As a general rule, many of these small fish feed on small invertebrates at night, and large fish eat small fish at dawn and dusk or schooling fish during the day. One exception to this rule is the tide pool sculpin. This small fish has a strong homing instinct to its tide pool, where it feeds on tiny invertebrates and scavenges dead animals day and night. Also present along rocky shores, especially among large boulders, are several eel-like fish that go by the imaginative names of gunnels, pricklebacks, cockscombs and warbonnets. Some of these fish are herbivores, but many eat shrimp, bryozoans, sponges, and tiny fish. In turn, they are important food items of many other fish, birds and marine mammals. The widespread and abundant high cockscomb is believed to be one of the many nocturnal inverte-brate eaters. It lurks among boulder-strewn beaches out of sight during the day. Schooling fish, like the shiner perch, will enter the intertidal regions of rocky shores to nibble at barnacles and mussels during day and night. This species gives birth to its young in calm bays, especially among eelgrass meadows, but will often be seen in large languid schools along rocky shores in summer. It is one of many fishes eaten by loons, cormorants, herons, and eagles as well as rockfish and lingcod.

In the subtidal reaches of the rocky shore live a diverse and colorful group of rockfish that include schooling species, solitary feeders, and fast and slow swimmers.[15] Over 330 species of rockfish live worldwide, and they are among the most common fish along the Pacific Coast. Kelp forests are especially favored by rockfish as places to feed, hide from predators, and reproduce.[15] The many shapes and sizes of rockfish reflect the diversity of prey items they eat. The greenling, yellowtail, black and quillback rockfish are the most numerous species in Puget Sound. Some species, such as the copper rockfish and the quillback, are stay-at-homes that lurk about rocky shores, darting out only to catch crabs, shrimps and small fishes. The schooling black rockfish and yellow rockfish, on the other hand, pursue schools of active small fish such as herring, sandlance and small shrimp. Rockfish give birth to live young from

February to September, depending on the species and location. Young rockfish specialize in a diet of invertebrates, and adult rockfish eat other fish and large invertebrates.

Most large rockfish feed in the low light of dawn and dusk. About thirty minutes after sunset, young rockfish, ratfish and sailfin sculpin emerge to feed on invertebrates through the night. Kelp greenling is the large predatory fish that feeds during the day, resulting in the greenling frequently falling prey to otters and seals. However, it is still among the most numerous species of rockfish that inhabit the rocky shore.

Topping my list of the most impressive rocky shore animals is the lingcod, the wolf eel and the giant Pacific octopus. Territorial in behavior, the lingcod is a formidable predator of young rockfish, squid and octopus. Huge matriarchs weighing over 30 kilograms (66 pounds) were present in the Strait of Georgia and Puget Sound until overfishing in the past few decades removed most of them. Lingcod are voracious feeders that emerge from hiding to snap at wounded and unsuspecting fish. They resemble mouths with a narrowing bag of a body streaming behind. Wolf eels live in rock crevices in the subtidal region where they stake out territories. Large specimens exceed 1 meter (3 feet) in length, and all possess formidable sets of teeth for dispatching clams, snails, and crabs. The giant Pacific octopus can exceed 25 kilograms (55 pounds) and reach over 3 meters (10 feet) in length. The major food in the octopus's diet is clams, but there are regional differences that partly reflect local abundance of particular species.[16] On the west coast of Vancouver Island, the diet is largely clams, particularly the cockle, the littleneck clam, and the Cancer crab. The octopus opens clams by exerting sheer force on the valves, or possibly by injecting venom through a tiny hole it drills with

The Jade Coast has an astonishing variety of rockfish. The yellow-eye and copper rockfish are sometimes numerous close to shore whereas the vermillion rockfish lurks in deep water (Danny Kent photos).

77

its rasping tongue-like appendage called a radula, which relaxes the clam, allowing it to be opened.[16]

Diving Predators

It is humbling to consider that the food web that links seaweed to limpets and snails is also tied to birds whose migrations will take them to the shores of mountain streams and boreal lakes in Canada or coral beaches of the South Pacific Islands. Many species of birds that spend part of their year along the rocky shores of the Jade Coast are important predators of rocky shore inverte- brates. Diving ducks are among the most conspicuous birds along the Pacific Coast in winter, when high tides allow them to dive for food during most of the day.[17] Most of the world's Barrow's goldeneye reside in winter along the Pacific Coast where they consume mussels and snails.

A most beautiful creature of the rocky shores is the harlequin duck. For most of its year, the harlequin dines from a smorgasbord of invertebrates pro- duced by the rocky shore food web – snails, limpets, small fish and their eggs, shrimp, urchins, mussels, barnacles and shorecrabs. Mated pairs depart the coast in May for breeding sites along the banks of fast-flowing mountain streams. Males return to the coast beginning in June followed later in summer

The Ups and Downs
of the Sea Otter

The sea otter has been protected from persecution since 1911, and it has since reoccupied about half of its historical range from Baja California to northern Japan. About 100,000 otters now reside in the north Pacific. A few hundred live on the Washington Coast, a few thou- sand in each of California and British Columbia, about 13,000 in Russia and about 74,000 in Alaska. The otter population is growing at a rate of about 19 percent per year in British Columbia – a rate near the maxi- mum achievable for this species. In California and Alaska the rate is much lower. Otters in the Aleutians and the Alaskan Peninsula are declin- ing for unknown reasons.[18]

by females and the young harlequins. The adults moult their flight and body feathers during summer and consequently are temporarily flightless.

The most numerous and widespread diving duck on rocky shores in winter is the surf scoter, which assembles in flocks of thousands or tens of thousands where herring spawn in spring. For the winter, scoters dine mostly on mussels that they wrestle free from rocks and on clams in sandy beaches that they reach during brief dives. Recent studies indicate that the surf scoter might be playing an important role in the presence and abundance of marine invertebrates in the calm-water regions of the Jade Coast. The surf scoter dives for mussels in flocks of hundreds or thousands of individuals. They dislodge mussels from their beds by tugging and twisting the bysus threads until they snap. One scoter eats about 13 square meters (137 square feet) of mussels over the winter and, by spring, the large flocks denude wide regions of previously populated mussels. The wholesale slaughter of mussels creates openings for other marine invertebrates that would otherwise be quite scarce on the Jade Coast.[19]

The lives of several mammals depend on rocky shore invertebrates, and the most celebrated species is the sea otter. Almost as well known as its fate at the hands of eighteenth and nineteenth century fur traders is the disruption the

The sea otter is rapidly colonizing its former haunts along the southern Jade Coast, and declining in parts of Alaska. Why it is doing well in the south and poorly in the north is a mystery (Mark Hobson photo).

removal of the sea otter had on the food chain of the Jade Coast rocky shore. The food chain of the sea otter is short: sea otters dine on sea urchins that eat kelp. With the extirpation of the sea otter from the Pacific Coast, sea urchins prospered by devouring kelp. This part of the story has been publicized far and wide. However, there is much more to this story. Where sea otters have been introduced in low densities, the abundance of invertebrates decline, and gulls begin to eat less favored mussels, whelks and barnacles. And where sea otters are very numerous, invertebrates are scarce and gulls prey on small fish. Thus, the diet of the gulls becomes narrower with increasing abundance of sea otters. Archaeologists unearthing centuries of discarded food items of the Aleuts on Amchitka Island in Alaska made a startling discovery. When sea otters were scarce, the shells of sea urchins and limpets littered the garbage heaps of the Aleuts, but when sea otters remains were present, limpets and sea urchins became scarce.[20]

Near the end of the food chains on rocky shores are many of the most charismatic species of the Pacific Coast. The fish eaters include the orca, bald eagle, and Steller's sea lion. In British Columbia, there are about 305 orcas that feed largely on salmon and 170 that eat mostly marine mammals.[21] The salmon-eating orcas assemble in Johnstone Strait and Juan de Fuca Strait in mid-June through autumn to intercept salmon returning to the Fraser River to spawn. These orcas reside along the coast for most of the summer. A second group of about 170 orcas steal quietly through coastal waters in pursuit of marine mammals. The harbor seal makes up over 50 percent of their diet followed by porpoises, sea lions, seabirds and the occasional deer. A third group of 200 or more individuals live offshore along the continental shelf. Little is known about their biology or their diet.

Eagles eat an astonishing array of animals, including fish, birds, mammals and invertebrates. One study looking at thirty-five eagle nests in the Strait of Georgia found evidence of a total of sixteen species of birds, four species of mammals, eleven species of fish, six species of shellfish, and four species of crabs.[22] Eagles use their talons to seize live and dead prey from water. Among the eagles' favored fishing sites are channels, where fish become stunned by eddies that rapidly bring them to the surface and where seabirds gather in large flocks. When an eagle begins to pursue seabirds, its actions signal its intent to all birds in the neighborhood. The direct and powerful flight sends squeals among fleeing gulls, ducks and seabirds. The intended victim will be pursued for short distances until it drops exhausted to the water or escapes from the eagle. There are a few thousand eagles in California, Oregon and Washington, about 9000 in British Columbia and 10,000 in southeast Alaska.

The most numerous and ubiquitous marine mammal along the shores of the Pacific Coast is the harbor seal. It tends to be a solitary feeder of crustaceans and fish. Herring, tomcod, hake, sculpins, cod, shiner perch, flounders, salmon, octopi, whelks and amphipods are some examples of its prey. Recently weaned seals eat mostly shrimp during the first few months of life.[23] The largest haul out in the world was on Tugidak Island in the Gulf of Alaska where over 20,000 seals were reported in the 1960s. Their numbers have since dwindled to a few thousand for reasons yet unknown.

The California sea lion and Steller sea lion are also fish eaters that haul out on rocky headlands and islets. Steller sea lions occur along the entire Jade Coast. Breeding rookeries span the length of the Jade Coast. The California sea lion breeds on islands in California; non-breeding animals are seen as far north as British Columbia. The number of California sea lions increased dramatically over the last century from a few thousand animals in the 1920s to about 14,000 in 1995. The cessation of commercial hunting in the early 1940s allowed the populations to gradually recover. Since protection was afforded the species in 1972, the California sea lion population along the Jade Coast has increased by about 5 percent per year.

The major breeding sites for California sea lions are the Channel Islands, San Nicolas, San Miguel, and San Clemente islands and islands in Baja California. Following pupping in May and June and breeding in July, most males migrate northward along the Jade Coast as far north as British Columbia. Large numbers arrive in February in British Columbia waters to dine on spawning herring. Resident sea lions in southern California tend to be females, pups and immatures.

The abundance of animals on rocky shores is not confined to the wave washed outer coast. Animals unable to withstand the pounding surf and low tide exposure to air and predators can find shelter between boulders and stones, or bury themselves in sand. This is the topic of the next chapter.

Plants and animals that live on Pacific sand beaches mostly live out of sight buried out of reach of dessication by wind, pounding surf and radiation from the sun. (Worth Spit, Coos Bay, Oregon.)

CHAPTER 5

Gravel and Sand

Touching the beach, they tumble in a roar lost in a general noise of storm.
Trampled by the wind and everlastingly moved and lifted up and flung down by
the incoming seas, the water offshore becomes a furious glassiness of marbly foam; wild,
rushing sheets of seethe fifty feet wide border it; the water streams with sand.
– Henry Beston, *The Outermost House*, 1928

The westerly wind announces its arrival along the Jade Coast with a rhythm that reaches into our soul. Its pounding beat sprints down the sand beach, endlessly swirling the grains of sand in a deluge of water. The sand beach never sleeps. Creatures inhabiting this shifting habitat must contend with regular burying and exposure. Where the sand becomes gravel, organisms must be able to deal with the added assault of a hail of stones tossed about by the surf. But where the sea is calm, gravel and sand can provide a foothold for a garden of seaweeds and shelter for creatures during low tides. Sand and gravel beaches are the home of many clams. They range from the high-speed razor clam to the long-lived, slow-moving geoduck. The abundance of clams attracts a host of clam eaters, including many familiar beach animals such as red rock crabs, sea stars, sea ducks, otters, black bears, and the seashore specialist, the northwestern crow, which has learned how to crack open clam shells on rocks.

The Nuts and Bolts of Gravel and Sand Environments

One of the first things you will notice when you step on to a gravel or sand beach is that some are covered in sea life while others are devoid of living things. The simple explanation is the action of waves. Beaches exposed to surf are often covered in barren, rounded rocks or clean, washed sand, whereas beaches away from the surf are often coated by seaweeds and abound with creatures beneath the stones or buried in the sand. Where the wave action is low or the boulders are sufficiently large that they do not move, many of the plants and animals found on rocky shores will be present. Immobile boulders and cobbles become an anchor for seaweeds and sessile animals, and the retiring species can find some safety in spaces beneath the rocks. Seaweeds cling to the tops of boulders while underneath the rocks are starfish, snails, crabs and anemones. In the rough and tumble world of unstable beaches, however, the rocks have a powdery feel to them from pulverizing one another when surf hits the beach. Few creatures can withstand the hail of rocks where wave action dislodges the boulders. But even there, a few animals survive by burying deep in the gravel.

Sand beaches are relatively rare along the Jade Coast, and the creatures that inhabit them must be able to withstand the shifting movement. Sand is a protective medium against the onslaught of heavy surf, so some soft-bodied creatures can survive on sand beaches but not on gravel beaches. Here the ability to move quickly through the shifting sand is an asset over the ability to cling to hard, solid surfaces of boulders. Thus, mussels, limpets and snails found on rocky shores and boulders are absent from pure sand beaches, which are inhabited instead by clams, worms and burying sea anemones.

Gravel and Sand Shore Food Webs

The physical effects of shifting sand and gravel play a vital role in which plants and animals are found along the beach. Where there is frequent scouring by sand and gravel, seaweeds are scarce, and most animals burrow out of sight. The source of food is largely from plankton that filters between sand grains and stones. In calm water, algae such as sea lettuce and kelps can cloak sand and gravel beaches. Together, plankton and seaweed are the primary producers of food. Grazing snails such as periwinkles and filter-feeding clams such as the little-neck clam are the first line of consumers. Predators such as the moon snail, staghorn sculpin and the northwestern crow eat clams, and the bald eagle consumes crows and fish. Along sandy shores washed by the surf, several worms fill the role of consumer, scavenger and predator, and the dainty sanderling eats all of them. Lastly, there is the clean-up crew that eats dead plants and animals.

THE PRODUCERS: PLANKTON AND SEAWEEDS

The sources of food for animals along gravel and sand beaches are plankton and seaweeds. Even clean-looking beaches contain tiny plants hidden between the grains of sand. Many of the seaweeds that live on rocky shores can also get a foothold on gravel and boulder beaches if the water is calm. Boulders offer a foothold for kelps, sargassum and rockweeds. Some conspicuous species include the Turkish towel, which has a texture resembling a rough towel. Its reddish color when alive fades to a pale yellow as it begins to deteriorate. The edible red laver or dulse is usually present along gravel shores near the low tide along with the iridescent kelp. Also present in the tangled garden are sugar kelp, alaria and seersucker. Sargassum forms tangled mats in deep water, and sea lettuce flourishes in calm locations.

Sand beaches contain many microscopic plants and bacteria that are the food of tiny animals not easily seen and largely unstudied. A few species seem to depend on burial. *Gymnogongrus linearis* is a red algae that rapidly grows through the spring in preparation for a summer burial.

GRAZERS

Many of the grazing species we met on rocky shores are also present on boulders, including limpets, barnacles, periwinkles, whelks and chitons. One of the most beautiful of intertidal starfish is the bat star. They come in a wide assortment of colors, and some are outlined with contrasting trim. Bat stars eat seaweeds, prey on sea urchins and scavenge dead animals but they do not eat clams or mussels.

SCAVENGERS AND DETRITUS FEEDERS

Sand beaches are scavenged by crabs, worms and other invertebrates. Among the most attractive scavengers is the shimmering olive snail, which searches for detritus just beneath the sand surface. A group of detritus feeders are the tiny opossum shrimp (or *Mysids*) and amphipods, which live in the top few centimetres (one inch) of sand.[1] Also present in this habitat is the tiny mole crab, which lives in small colonies that form dimples in the sand. Mole crabs eat detritus that is deposited by retreating

Boarders in the Burrow

A commensal pea crab, a scale worm, a tiny clam, a small fish and an isopod inhabit the burrows of the ghost shrimp. None of these creatures has a home if its own, and all are boarders in the shrimp's home.

waves. Their presence along the Jade Coast is thought to depend on the frequency with which north-flowing ocean currents deposit larvae from points farther south.[2] Isopods are also present between the sand grains. They live by scavenging carcasses of fish and other invertebrates. A species that announces its presence with an exceedingly annoying bite on bare feet at the edge of the water is the water-line isopod *Excirolana kincaidi.* Bloodworms, like their terrestrial counterparts the earthworms, eat sand grains to absorb the associated nourishment. Bloodworms can be very plentiful in places and often become the object of a tug-of-war for shorebirds.

Among the most conspicuous of detritus feeders are the beach hoppers, which live in and under piles of decomposing seaweed. Another conspicuous detritus eater is the sand dollar. Sand dollars cash in on the detritus littering the beach. They use tiny black hairs on their shells to deflect detritus toward the mouth pore by orienting themselves at an angle to the beach and away from the prevailing ocean current. This behavior probably exposes more surface area to the water and improves the chances of catching and processing particles of food.

Where the sand has a mixture of mud, miniature volcanoes often pock mark the surface. These are the burrow entrances to the retiring ghost and mud shrimps. The ghost shrimp shimmers in a satin pink shell. It moves toward the entrance as the tide floods the beach to nibble on bits of seaweed. The mud shrimp looks like it has turned blue in the cold water. It generally prefers muddier locations and builds less distinct "volcano" entrances than the ghost shrimp.

Burrowing Filter Feeders

When dropped on wet sand, the powerful foot goes into its digging routine with movements so swift the eye can hardly follow them. A razor clam has been observed to flip itself upright and completely disappear below the surface in seven seconds – Euell Gibbons, *Stalking the Blue-eyed Scallop*

The wide-open surf-washed beaches of the Jade Coast appear to be deserts, but living just below the surface are several creatures with remarkable behaviors. One of my all-time favorites is the sprinter among clams—the razor clam. Its siphon tips barely break the sand surface. Its razor-thin shells are streamlined into fine racing form. The razor clam's remarkable speed is a result of a

Clams That Flip Out

The basket cockle has an escape routine from the predatory sunflower star, *Pycnopodia*, that is truly remarkable. When the tentacles of a sunflower star make contact with the flesh of a cockle, the clam extends its foot and violently flips itself out of reach of the star.

retractable foot that it pushes through the sand and inflates to pull itself into the sand. Razor clams feed by filtering plankton from seawater through an extendible siphon when the tide floods the beach.

Clams come into their own on the sand and gravel beaches of the Jade Coast. There are over 200 species on the Jade Coast, but only a few species are numerous. The sand clam lies buried in clean sand, where it vacuums the surface with a long siphon. A close relative is the soft-shelled clam. This highly prized species was introduced to the Jade Coast from the Atlantic Coast about a century ago where it is known as the steamer or long-necked clam. The bent-nosed clam resembles the sand clam but has a bend in the tip of the shell and prefers muddy conditions. In quiet stretches of sand and gravel beaches, the horse clam and geoduck announce their presence by spitting water into the air. With shells up to 15 centimeters (6 inches) long, the geoduck is one of the largest burying bivalves in the world.[3] These huge clams reside several centimeters below the surface of the beach and far from the reach of predators. When it is mealtime, they extend a long siphon through the substrate until it reaches the seawater. Then, by puffing and blowing like a cigar smoker, they inhale plankton from the water and extrude wastes. At the opposite extreme are the littleneck clams that live just below the surface of gravel beaches, and the slightly deeper-dwelling butter clam. The latter three species are frequent fare in West Coast chowders.

Most clams reside in the relatively sanguine habitat below the surface of the sand. However, the basket cockle is the rebel of the group – it has taken to living on the surface of the sand and mud beaches. To live such an exposed life style, the basket cockle jettisoned the long siphon of other clams, perhaps because crabs would make short order of it. The cockle also has a strongly ribbed shell to thwart the crab's powerful pincers. The larvae settle below the low tide where they grow until, with the help of a strong single foot and a rugged shell, they storm the beach.

PREDATORS

Burrowing Predators

In Greek mythology, sea-maidens known as Nereids had prophetic abilities, and lucky was the sailor who could catch one. The clam worm, pile worm or sand worm known as *Nereis* can be found in sand, gravel, rock and surf-washed beaches but it is usually encountered on gravel beaches. The clam worm is an iridescent reddish brown color with short appendages on the length of its body that help it move about. It also sports a mean-looking set of biting parts that it opens and closes in an impressive display of anger when handled.

Sand beaches are home to predatory worms such as the thin, ribbon-like *Cerebratulus* and the multi-legged *Nephtys,* which prey on other burying worms. They also house a particularly voracious clam predator called the bull-dozing moon snail. It carries a heavy round shell on a bulging foot so large that it engulfs part of the shell. It would seem impossible for the moon snail to retract such a huge appendage into its shell but given enough encouragement, the snail ejects water and withdraws behind a leathery trap door known as an

Orgy under the Full Moon

Whatever the clamworm loses in the way of beauty, it makes up by the remarkable orgy it performs on summer nights when the moon is full. During mating, the posterior segments containing the gonads swell with sperm or eggs, and the tiny legs become small paddles. As the flood tide approaches its zenith, the clamworm emerges from the sediment to dance beneath the moon. Seemingly unconcerned for its safety, the male writhes through the water spewing sperm as he goes. This dance is too much for the females to resist, and they soon emerge to scatter eggs through the water.

A moon snail half submerged in loose gravel bulldozes its way through a gravel beach in search of clams.

operculum. The first evidence of the presence of moon snails on a beach is often their collar-shaped egg cases. The tiny eggs are extruded into a mucous that mixes and binds with sand that the snail emits as it turns. The resulting collar-shaped egg case is discarded on the surface of the beach. The young moon snails will hatch into free-swimming larvae to join the plankton soup in mid-summer before settling to grow into the adult form.

Surface Predators

In the northern reach of the Strait of Georgia lies Mitlenatch Island. Mitlenatch is among the smaller of the islands in the Strait, but its natural features make it remarkably different. The island is largely exposed rock with grassy meadows and copses of shrubs and trees, and its isolation makes it attractive to nesting birds. About 2000 pairs of gulls, several hundred cormorants and guillemots, and about 60 pairs of northwestern crows nest there each summer. Very little was known about this Pacific seashore crow and, in 1976, I decided to change all that. I began a three-year study into the social behavior of crows that formed the basis of a graduate degree.[4]

Researching animals often turns up surprises and reveals our own short-comings. Most birds can be watched near their nests from a canvas shelter known as a bird blind. The trick is to have a companion accompany you into the blind and then depart alone. Most birds can't count and although they are puzzled for a short while over the presence of a structure nearby, soon the urge to return to the nest overcomes their fear and life goes on as if nothing has changed. But I knew that crows would be too smart for this trick. So I decided to try to find a site where I could come and go without being noticed by the crows. After all, the human mind should be able to outsmart that of a crow.

I watched crows come and go from the beach for about thirty minutes before I had located three nests. The best location was a nest in an isolated willow on a rocky bluff overlooking a large meadow. I tucked the rolled-up canvas bird blind beneath my arm and trudged up the hill to near the nest. At about 50 meters (160 feet) away, a crow let out an alarm call that brought its mate from the beach to pelt me with insults. Clearly, they would not let me get near that nest.

For the next few days, I scrambled over rocks, crawled through shrubs, tore my jeans on blackberry barbs, and generally got beaten up searching for crow nests. My ordeal had provided me with the locations of about thirty nests. One nest was located in a nine-bark shrub along a gully where I plotted to install the blind. The location was perfect. I could steal into the shrubs and scurry along the gully out of sight of all the crows. But first I had to install the blind without the crows becoming suspicious. I had to be patient; my plan was to time my arrival to coincide with the brief period that the parents were away from the nest.

The day arrived bright and sunny. The shadows in the gully reflected blue on the basalt and would help camouflage the blind. I waited from a vantage point on a rocky bluff for about thirty minutes before the crow slipped from her nest. She flew to a nearby rock, looked about, and then departed for the beach about 300 meters (975 feet) away. I ducked into the shrubs to hurry along the gully like a thief in the night. The nest was vacant just below the canopy, and I could see three eggs lying in the cedar-bark lined nest. It was perfect. Within a few minutes, the blind was in place. I slipped inside, checked that the canvas window flaps were closed, and scampered out the rear door and up the gully. From the nest, the blind completely obscured my approach and exit along the gully.

The sunlight hurt my eyes when I emerged from the shrubbery at the far end of the copse. As I squinted toward the nest, one of the crows returned to the rocky meadow near its nest. It had worked. The blind was in place without the crow's knowledge. I lifted my binoculars to watch as she alighted on a branch near her nest. She was disturbed by the presence of the blind and it took sever-al flights to and from the vicinity of the nest before she slipped back to her nest. Now all I had to do was wait for the crows to habituate to the presence of the blind, and return to begin to follow the crows' nesting activities in detail.

The next day broke sunny and warm. The tide was low, and crows were shuttling to and from nests and the beach. I decided that this was the day to return to the blind. A few crows scoffed as I scaled the hillside, and the gulls' paranoid shrieks filled the air. I checked that my notebook was secure in my pocket and slipped my binocular strap over one arm the way a bandito might carry strings of bullets. Into the shadows I crept. My heart was pounding, and I hardly uttered a breath. As a boy, I had learned how to walk in the woods with-out making a sound by carefully rolling the bottom of my foot on the ground. I held my breath as I slid through the doorway of the bird blind, proud that I had not made a sound. I found a comfortable place to sit and opened my note-book. I entered the date, the nest and the time of day. The moment of reckon-ing had arrived.

Although the wind over the island was cool, the gully lay sheltered beneath a blanket of still air. The perspiration trickled down my forehead and dropped off my nose. It was sweltering in the blind. I opened a window flap on the side of the blind away from the view of the crow's nest to allow some air circulation. Then, ever so slowly, I opened the window flap closest to the nest. A tiny shaft of light burst through the crack and through the slit I saw that the nest was empty. A sudden fear overcame me that the crows had abandoned the nest. Only time would tell. If the crows were on the beach, they should return in about ten minutes.

The minutes ticked by and no crows were seen. Gulls squealed at their nests only a few meters away and out of sight behind a wall of leaves.

Abruptly, a flapping of wings hit the canopy. I froze. I could hear the crow but I couldn't see her through the tiny window slit of the blind. She was mov-ing about in the shrubs, and I was poised to start observing her at the nest. I checked my watch and noted the time in my book.

Now there comes a time in everyone's life when the universe does not unfold as expected. It is as if all the careful planning and implementation was a conspiracy by some higher order to expose our frailties. It is what parents refer to as character building.

Jade Coast Crows and Gulls

The northwestern crow and glaucous-winged gull are endemic to the Jade Coast. Crows nest in trees, shrubs, on the ground and alongside nesting gulls on small islands. The crow has a distinctively harsh *kar-kar-kar* call. The gull is believed to have evolved along the edge of the retreating ice sheet over 12,000 years ago.[5] Whereas the crow is restricted to foraging on the beach, the gull is able to wade, swim or dive for fish in the shallows.

Crows have a particularly loud call that they use to advertise their presence. Even on a windy day, they can be heard tossing insults to one another. I had never heard this call less than a meter (3 feet) from my ear, and its first shrill note nearly knocked me over. I sprung from the ground and hit my head on the canvas roof, uprooting one of the guy lines. The blind teetered as a pole fell toward me. From not more than a meter (3 feet) away, the crow was shrieking at me from the end window of the blind. Within a few seconds, its mate was into the thicket and others were assembling along the copse. With ringing condemnation raining upon me, I collapsed the blind and made my way back up the gully. Emerging at the far end, I came upon a caucus of crows whose verdict was clear. My fate was sealed. From now on, I would have to watch crows from afar through a telescope and binoculars. The bedroom activities of crows would remain a secret, and I turned my attention to their behavior on the beach.

It is nearly impossible to walk onto a gravel beach along the northern Jade Coast without being announced by a northwestern crow or glaucous-winged gull. Most gravel and sand beaches have a party of crows and gulls that argue over who will have first access to scavenge and prey on a smorgasbord of animals that inhabit the intertidal area. The diet of both species is largely opportunistic and therefore varies by location.[4] Widespread species such as shorecrabs, clams, gunnels and snails are prominent items on the menu of crows, and gulls add larger crabs and fish carcasses that are not stolen away by the clever crow. The larger size of the gull allows it to bully the wily crow.

Other bird predators inhabiting the sand beaches are sanderlings, which resemble small windup toys scampering before the surf. Flocks of sanderlings probe the clean sand in search of mole crabs and small worms. The sanderling's preference for running rather than flying is probably to save energy. Sanderlings breed in the high arctic archipelago of Canada and spend the winter on sandy beaches from the Queen Charlotte Islands to Tierra del Fuego. Why some migrate a few thousand kilometers(few thousand miles) while others fly to the most distant tip of South America is a mystery.

Finding a sea star can be a highlight of a visit to the beach. The mottled star (left) is slowly opening a clam to become a meal. The morning star (right) is a predator of other sea stars.

Small parties of semipalmated plovers also hunt worms in the sand beaches. However, whereas the sanderling relies on touch receptors in its bill to detect worms, the plover watches for slight movements in the sand and runs to the spot to pull the worms from the beach. Other shorebirds that put in an appearance along sand beaches include the western sandpiper, least sandpiper, whimbrel, short-billed and long-billed dowitchers, and bald eagles. We often think of the bald eagle as a predator, but it is largely a scavenger of animals that die along our shores. The eagle eats mostly scavenged fish but also hunts gulls, ducks and live fish.

Beneath the rocks of the gravel beach dwell a few conspicuous animals. Overturning the rocks will sometime reveal a wriggling fish that resembles an eel. A widespread species is the cockscomb prickleback. This species hides under rocks by day to emerge at nighttime to eat small invertebrates brought inshore by flood tides. Very numerous along gravel beaches of the Jade Coast is the purple shorecrab, a small crab that fits into the palm of your hand with room to spare. Shorecrabs live beneath nearly every large rock on the beach and prey on small invertebrates; scavenge dead fish, clams, mussels and other animals; and nibble at seaweeds. I have often wondered why the small and presumably young, shorecrabs come in a kaleidoscope of colors and patterns whereas the larger, older crabs are so similar.

Gravel beaches are also the domain of some voracious sea stars. The sunflower star is the largest sea star you will likely encounter. It has up to twenty-four arms with a reach nearly half a meter (16 inches) across. The sunflower star is a predator of sea urchins, hermit crabs, sea cucumbers, clams and sand dollars, which it pursues with surprising speed. Abalones, scallops and anemones show bizarre writhing escape routines to distance themselves from this voracious killer. But there are worse things lurking in the depths. The morning sun star is a fierce predator of other starfish and a cannibal. In Puget Sound and the Strait of Georgia, the morning sun star eats the sun stars and leather stars. Its close relative, the sun star, is also a carnivore but directs its attention most often toward sea cucumbers, sea squirts and sea pens.

Swimming Predators

A flooding tide brings with it a new shift of predatory fish, ducks and mammals eager to snatch up worms, small fish and clams. The staghorn sculpin and the sand sole follow the tide in search of unsuspecting worms, clams, small fish and generally any animal they can get into their mouths. They are widespread species on gravel, mud and sand beaches, in estuaries and eelgrass meadows.

In the fine, silvery sand lining many bays along the Pacific Coast dwell *Ampeliscid* amphipods that eat detritus arriving from the seashore. These amphipods are especially important food items for a very large predator, the gray whale. An amphipod produces distinctive tubes that jut out of the sand and are especially tantalizing to gray whales.[6] Gray whales are unique among the baleen whales in that they feed by suctioning their prey from the silt through the sides of their mouth and sifting out food items with the baleen. Craters in the seafloor are a telltale sign of the presence of gray whales. A 12-meter (40-foot) whale is estimated to eat 552 kilograms of amphipods and other invertebrates in twelve hours.[6] The unwitting actions of gray whales create the craters favored by its prey, the amphipod.[7]

Clams, mussels, snails and barnacles are the mainstay in the diet of huge numbers of sea ducks that spend the winter along the Jade Coast. Scoters, goldeneyes and bufflehead ducks can reach or dive for clams, snails and barnacles along the intertidal portion of beaches on the Jade Coast in winter because tides are high for most of the day. The principal species are the surf, white-winged and black scoters, Barrow's and common goldeneyes, and the bufflehead. Often these ducks will come within few meters (few yards) of the shore in search of food. During summer, the tides are mostly low during the day so the sea ducks depart the coast to breed in the boreal forest or on the arctic tundra. Buffleheads are usually solitary feeders whereas scoters and goldeneyes are gregarious. Flocks of fewer than a few hundred birds are typically found, but in particularly rich feeding areas, flocks can numbers in the thousands.

The abundance of fish, crabs and clams on gravel beaches attract a few carnivorous mammals. The river otter is equally at home in the sea as in the river. Along the Jade Coast, the river otter dives for fish, crabs and clams along gravel and sand beaches. Otters den among logs, cracks in rocks and in underground burrows, and leave scent markings and droppings on rocky points, docks, and driftwood logs. Less conspicuous but equally widespread is the mink. This small weasel is closely associated with water, where it lives largely on crabs. At one time the black bear roamed the entire length of the Jade Coast, but humans have excluded it from many of its former coastal haunts. However, on remote stretches of the Jade Coast, black bears still frequent beaches to hunt shorecrabs, clams and stranded fish. Black bears are numerous along remote parts of the coast. The raccoon frequents the shoreline of the Jade Coast as far north as British Columbia. It was introduced in the last century to the Queen Charlotte Islands. Racoons have a catholic diet and find the shellfish, crabs, seabirds and fish on the seashore to their liking.

In some places where the land braces against the onslaught of the ocean, the sand takes on a permanency and provides a toehold for the establishment of a sinewy plant known as eelgrass. The next chapter explores the undersea gardens that thrive in eelgrass meadows.

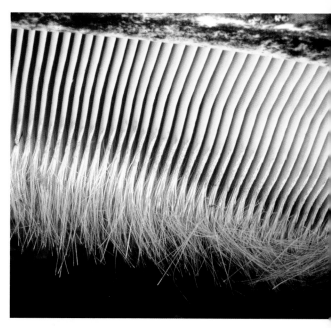

Baleen hanging from the roof of the mouth of a gray whale sieves invertebrates from the mud that it slurps from sandy shores of the Jade Coast. (Austin Reed)

Although the Jade Coast is deluged with rain, large deltas such as this one at the mouth of the Stikine River, are few and far between.

CHAPTER 6

Eelgrass Meadows and Salt Marsh

Strange it is how things work out sometimes. A man starts out for a place in mind, but before
he gets there he comes on something more to his liking than he thought a spot ever could be.
That's how it was with Cache Lake.

– John J. Rowlands, *Cache Lake Country: Life in the North Woods*

When I was a young boy, I stumbled upon John J. Rowlands's book *Cache Lake Country: Life in the North Woods*. It told of Rowlands's years at the helm of a canoe in summer in the north and in a log cabin in winter. It was a dream world for a boy, and I used to lie awake at nights dreaming of taking to the north woods in my own canoe to seek my Cache Lake.

There are many larger eelgrass meadows along the Jade Coast than on Sidney Lagoon in the Canadian Gulf Islands but it was the 40-hectare (98-acre) meadow in Sidney Lagoon that became my Cache Lake. Scientists are curious people and, admittedly, sometimes a little odd, and the field biologist ranks high on both scores. Any opportunity to explore new territory or to see new species is taken up with relish.

And so it was that in 1985, I entered the shallow lagoon on Sidney Island. I had spent many summers working on islands and found the lure of a lagoon on an island irresistible. Scores of herons fed in the shallows. The falling tide had exposed the mudflat and as I slowly motored deeper into the lagoon, I made a mental note to return later in the summer to study shorebirds. At the southeastern shore I went ashore.

A narrow band of pickleweed and spikegrass was halted abruptly by second-growth alder, grand fir, cedar and arbutus. The forest was eerily silent. The dead leaves of alders crunched underfoot and off in the distance a small herd of fallow deer thundered deeper into the woods. The trees swayed in the wind and a flycatcher called overhead.

Years of field work hones the senses – the eye catches a faint movement, the ear picks up a distant animal's chirp, and the nose recognizes the unmistakable smell of guano. Across the breeze lay the smell of bird shit. Like a bloodhound on the scent, I was off along an abandoned skid road where a donkey engine had dragged immense Douglas firs to the shore years earlier. Within two minutes, I had tracked the spoor to a cluster of heron nests swaying top-heavy in thin alders. The nesting colony had abandoned the site, but not before laying eggs. Eggshells littered the ground. Something had put the herons off their nests, and ravens and crows were quick to gobble up the eggs.

I returned in July to camp on the northern shore in Sidney Spit Marine Park and boated across the lagoon entrance to watch and band migrant shorebirds. Tiny western sandpipers were very numerous and, with the help of three assistants, I managed to catch about eighty-five birds in a few days. Each bird was weighed and measured, and got a unique combination of color bands before being released. I then began a regular search to determine how long they stayed. Most stayed for only a few days. While I was busy banding and observing shorebirds, I noted that herons were numerous in the lagoon. They had probably started to nest once more in the alder forest at the far end of the lagoon.

Concern was mounting about the potential problems of chemical contaminants in many animals in Canada, including herons, and in 1986, I began to investigate their nesting success around the Strait of Georgia. It soon became apparent that some herons carried very high levels of some dioxin isomers, and research on herons began in earnest. This was a chance to work on Sidney Island where I believed herons would be little affected by chemical contaminants from distant pulp mills.

I proceeded to build a small cabin on Sidney Island. It was important that the cabin be quickly built so I could get on with watching herons, so I arranged for a carpenter to construct a 5 meter by 8 meter (12 foot by 20 foot) building held together by bolts.

The unassembled building was transported to the south beach on a barge where it was off-loaded above the high tide line. The walls were thin plywood and the roof was asphalt shingles. My assistant Terry Sullivan and I toted bricks from the nearby woods to build a footing. The floor and wall panels were quickly bolted into place, the joists carefully positioned, and the roofing was nailed in place. On the second day, we added the door, asphalt shingles and cabin furniture. The Spartan cabin had four small windows, one facing the South Beach, one to the west, and two overlooking the lagoon. And so began a decade of research.

Mudflats harbor many intriguing animals, especially if they are covered by meadows of eelgrass. Eelgrass meadows are the antithesis of the rocky shore. They are marine gardens where life is serene, fecund and fragile. There is little need for the strong holdfasts or rugged shells required to withstand the thunderous waves of the exposed coast.

In stark contrast to the stability of eelgrass meadows, salt marshes are demanding places where shifting soil, persistent winds, searing heat, ice, rain and salt spray challenge the tenacity of flora and fauna. Many salt marsh creatures have wide environmental tolerances to enable them to straddle this halfway house between marine and terrestrial lifestyles.

We live in the shadow of our ancestors' decisions, which are not always appropriate to our times. The abhorrence of mudflats that began a century ago has been played out in many of the salt marshes on the Pacific Coast. With the arrival of the plough, the drainage ditch and the dike, bays and deltas near human settlements suffered the greatest loss – 90 percent of salt marshes in the Coos Bay salt marsh, 60 percent in Puget Sound and 99 percent on the Fraser River delta. Fragments of the once widespread salt marshes can be found on the margins of Boundary Bay on the Fraser River delta, British Columbia, and in Coos Bay, Yaquina Bay and Tillamook Bay in Oregon. The real tragedy is that so little was known about salt marsh ecosystems that many of its secrets might have been extinguished in the haste to dyke and till the soil.

The Nuts and Bolts of Eelgrass Meadows and Salt Marshes

Eelgrass meadows straddle the intertidal and subtidal regions, whereas salt marshes lie between the terrestrial and intertidal. Sea temperature and clarity of water limit where eelgrass meadows will grow. Distinct zones of different vegetation outline the level of sea submergence in the salt marsh, but the

Eelgrass meadows straddle the bottom of the beach and the subtidal such as on Salt Spring Island, British Columbia, and salt marshes grow at the top of the beach. A particularly fine example is on Sidney Island, British Columbia.

amount of moisture, salinity and nutrients in the sediments also dictate their distribution.

SEA TEMPERATURE AND SUNLIGHT

Sea temperature and sunlight trigger photosynthesis in eelgrass meadows, which sends a chain of events rippling through the entire ecosystem. Sunlight warms the beaches at low tide and moderates the surrounding sea temperature. The amount of sunlight reaching the eelgrass plants determines how far down the beach they can grow. There is an important conservation message here: turbid waters caused by events such as oil spills, sewage, and plankton blooms can reduce the growth of eelgrass. And, as we will see, without eelgrass the entire ecosystem would collapse.

SALINITY

Eelgrass is tolerant of a wide range of salinity, but it does best where the water is brackish. The open ocean has a salinity of about thirty-five parts salt per thousand parts water; eelgrass grows best in water with a salinity between ten and thirty parts salt per thousand parts water. Any animal living in the intertidal zone has to cope with changes in salinity, which some do by moving in and out of the intertidal portion of the beach. But for plants, salinity is an invisible barrier; few terrestrial plants can tolerate saline conditions that sap them of precious moisture. So the competition for space goes to the salt-loving halophytes which have adapted to life in the salt zone. Many salt marsh plants store water in fleshy stems or roots, and grow tiny leaves covered with fine, glaucous hairs to reduce evaporation loss.

SEDIMENTS AND NUTRIENTS

Plant detritus by itself is not very nourishing. However, detritus is quickly coated by bacterial microbes that then become food for many invertebrates. A tiny detritus particle can pass many times between invertebrate to invertebrate as microbes repeatedly colonize the particle, only to have an invertebrate strip it bare. This process can be repeated over and over until eventually the remaining tiny detritus particles are eaten. The roots of eelgrass do much more than just anchor the plant in soft sediments. The shower of leaf litter from the floating canopy creates oxygen-depleted sediments about the roots where sulfur bacteria thrive. These bacterial microbes decompose detritus in the low-oxygen sediments by fermentation and give off hydrogen sulphide as byproduct.[1]

Salt marshes develop where high tides inundate low-lying land. Little is known about marsh soils in the Jade Coast region. The lower elevations are often saturated with moisture and are oxygen-poor just below the surface. The by-products of decomposition in these soils are toxic to some organisms, making an already harsh environment more rigorous for its inhabitants.

Eelgrass and Salt Marsh Food Webs

The producers inhabiting eelgrass meadows are phytoplankton, marine algae and eelgrass. They produce food energy through photosynthesis. The grazers include such animals as the chink shell, which grazes algae on eelgrass fronds, and the brant goose, which eats eelgrass fronds. Among the filter feeders are many small invertebrates that cling to eelgrass fronds and clams that live in the mud. The predators include invertebrates such as the Dungeness crab, birds such as the great blue heron, and fish. In sum, very dissimilar animals eat very similar food.

The producers that inhabit large salt marshes are glasswort and grasses such as spike grass and wild rye. The grazers are ducks such as the American wigeon and northern pintail.

THE PRODUCERS IN THE EELGRASS MEADOW AND SALT MARSH

Eelgrass Meadows

On sunny summer days, a green sheen of eelgrass shimmers in a mirage that stretches for kilometers along many of the great beaches of the Jade Coast. At low tide, the eelgrass looks like a meadow uncovered by the sea. Beach walkers will be familiar with the long sinuous green leaves of eelgrass sprouting from sandy beaches near the low tide. There are forty-eight species of seagrass in the world, of which five species live on the Jade Coast. Three of these are surfgrasses (*Phyllospadix*) found in rocky habitats exposed to Pacific surf. Two species of eelgrass are the widespread *Zostera marina,* which grows along the entire Pacific Coast, and a recent invader, the diminutive *Zostera japonica,* currently established on beaches to the south, including the Strait of Georgia. Particularly, large beds of eelgrass are found in Humboldt Bay, Netarts Bay, Willapa Bay, Grays Harbor, Padilla Bay, Boundary Bay, Tofino Inlet, Skidegate Inlet and Izembek Lagoon, Alaska. About 9 percent of Puget Sound below mean lower low water is covered by eelgrass.[2]

Eelgrasses are vascular plants that share features common to many terrestrial plants. They produce flowers, albeit tiny and inconspicuous ones, and have root-like underground rhizomes. The long narrow leaves slow the movement of water, and the tangles of rhizomes stabilize sediments that enrich the area around the plant. The long, swaying leaves also conceal tremendous numbers of animals that use the bed as a refuge and nursery. However, eelgrass provides much more to the ecosystem than just the breakdown products of its leaves.

One of the reasons that eelgrass habitats in tropical and temperate environments are so rich in species is that they provide many places for other plants and animals to grow. The leaves of eelgrass grow at an astonishing rate of about 5 millimeters (3/16 inch) each day and can reach up to 10 millimeters (3/8 inch) per day under ideal conditions. These leaves support a microcosm of epiphytic plants and animals, as well as provide food for grazing animals and supply detritus that feeds invertebrates in the eelgrass beds and on nearby beaches.

In Alaska eelgrass survives ice conditions but in Washington and California it cannot. Generally, eelgrass grows best when the surrounding sea is about 22 degrees Celsius (74 degrees Fahrenheit). Increasing sea temperatures in late winter triggers eelgrass reproduction as early as February.[3] Flowers can appear as early as March and as late as July. The growth of leaves begins in the warmth of July and extends into November.

Imagine how different we would feel if our lives were dependent on scum. At first glance, it is difficult to believe that the unappealing mass can be important – but it is the cornerstone to the life in eelgrass beds. Without the leaves of eelgrass, myriads of tiny plants, bacteria and diatoms that cling tenaciously to the leaves would be buried in mud or carried away by currents and tides. Within days, meter (39-inch) long leaves of eelgrass can turn a two-dimensional mudflat into a three-dimensional garden of plants and animals suspended in a watery environment rich with plankton. The weight of this growth on the leaves of eelgrass can be twice the weight of the leaves themselves![4]

The colonization of eelgrass leaves begins with settlement by diatoms and bacteria, and ends with the appearance of tiny algae.[4] Without the ability of these tiny organisms to rapidly colonize eelgrass leaves, much of the life of the eelgrass ecosystem would not survive. Entire life cycles of these epiphytic plants and animals are adapted to the three- to eight-week life span of eelgrass leaves. At first glance, the eelgrass appears to be getting the worst of the deal, but the relationship between epiphytes and eelgrass has evolved to be mutually benefi-cial. Eelgrass provides the epiphytes with a free ride suspended in nutrient-rich waters and close to the surface where the sun shines brightest. In return, the epi-phytes provide carbon, nitrogen and phosphorous to the eelgrass, which it needs to produce food.[5]

Suspended Gardens Another widespread plant in eelgrass meadows is a red alga *Smithora naiadum,* which clings to the edges of eelgrass leaves and is conspicuous because of its reddish purple hue. Also abundant are carnivorous amphipods, known as skeleton shrimp that resemble exuberant miniature preying mantids. Jellyfish and tiny sea anemones cling to eelgrass in summer.

One of the most remarkable creatures of eelgrass meadows is the hooded nudibranch. This creature is a predatory sea slug that reaches 10 centimeters (4 inches) in length and devours small amphipods and other crustaceans with the aid of a hood. It resembles a flaccid mass of jelly in the hand, but in the water the hooded nudibranch quickly fills out its hood and delicate-looking sacs. It uses the hood as a flotation device to drift to the surface and catch small crus-taceans with its tentacles. This animal wouldn't stand a chance on exposed rocky shores. Eugene Kozloff refers to the hooded nudibranch in his superb book *Seashore Life of the Northern Pacific Coast* as one of the "top ten" curiosi-ties brought to marine biologists, or described over the telephone. Another curiosity is the delicate-looking *Phyllaplysia taylori,* a yellow-green sea slug bearing longitudinal black streaks. A third sea slug in eelgrass meadows is the tiny *Aeolia papillosa,* which Kozloff aptly describes as resembling a shaggy little mouse. Its diet is largely, if not exclusively, anemones. Often crawling about the leaves of eelgrass is an isopod that takes on the color of its background. A con-spicuous group of clingers on are the sponges and hydroids. A tiny sessile jelly-fish measuring up to about two centimeters (one inch) and the graceful kelp crab also reside in eelgrass meadows. The jellyfish eats plankton and small crus-taceans, and the crab scavenges dead animals, often in association with broken-back and coon-striped shrimp.

Salt Marshes

The edge of the sea is a harsh environment for plants. One of the survivors is a fleshy-stemmed flowering plant known as glasswort, saltwort or pickleweed Two

The calm water bays along the Jade Coast are havens for hundreds of thousands of ducks and shorebirds. Mount Baker in Washington looms over Boundary Bay, British Columbia.

species of grass, saltgrass and arrow grass, are also widespread. Glasswort is the vanguard of the salt marsh progression down the beach. It forms slightly farther down the beach than the grasses, sometimes on partly rotted eelgrass windrows. Clumps of arrow grass often grow in areas of the marsh where silt collects.

Where the land is flat, a band of saltgrass often abruptly establishes landward of the glasswort. In summer, the sturdy dry stems of saltgrass deter all but the strongest bare feet from venturing far. The perennial seaside plantain also lives there, its green stems offering a welcome change from the monotonous expanse of duff-colored saltgrass. The plantain maintains its green color by storing energy reserves through the winter and thus is relished by waterfowl in spring. Higher along the beach, where only the highest tides reach, often grows a yellow daisy-like flowering plant known as gumweed, so-called for its sticky, white latex in the developing flower-heads. Its bright yellow petals make it one of the

Herbivorous Ducks

John Baldwin and Jim Lovvorn from the University of Wyoming estimated that 85 percent of the diet of wigeon in autumn was made up of the introduced species of eelgrass, *Zostera japonica*. By early winter, the ducks in British Columbia and Washington ate most of the eelgrass that had not washed ashore in storms, and then flew to neighboring farmlands to eat winter crops, weeds and invertebrates.[6]

showiest of salt marsh flora from June to November. Also in this part of the marsh is the silverweed, named for its silvery undersides. In some areas, silverweed can cover the ground in a near continuous mat of leaves. Both gumweed and silverweed show their affinity for terrestrial habitats by growing outside salt marshes too. At the top of the beach wild rye often grows in profusion.

GRAZERS

In the early 1990s, I began a study of the birds of Boundary Bay that opened my eyes to the importance of eelgrass beds to their survival. Autumn on the Jade Coast is a time when waterfowl are on the move. From Alaska, central British Columbia and Alberta, ducks and geese stream along the coast by the millions, and Boundary Bay is one of their favorite destinations. I drove my truck on to a dike that skirts along the top of the beach of Boundary Bay. From there I could see ducks stretching across a leaden sea to the horizon. Wigeon, pintails, teal and mallards were tipping and sieving the shallows for food. Scaup and scoters were in deeper water. Along the beach scampered thousands of dunlin and plovers. I wondered how I would ever estimate the number of birds that day. The ducks were milling about, but few were flying. The shorebirds were more mobile but generally stayed within view. By counting groups of fifty or 100, I could gradually tally the number on the beach. Over the next few hours, I alternated short drives with counts of flocks and eventually tallied nearly 100,000 ducks and 30,000 shorebirds.

Ducks and geese are the most conspicuous grazers of eelgrass meadows and salt marshes. Eelgrass meadows are one of the great storehouses of ducks in

Mallards are found in many habitats such as estuaries, beaches, rivers, lakes and farmlands.

winter along the Pacific. About 100,000 ducks congregate each winter on Boundary Bay; 50,000 gather in each of Grays Harbor, Padilla and Samish Bays; 200,000 amass in Willapa Bay and 124,000 collect in Humboldt Bay. Many small estuaries also harbor ducks, geese, swans and other waterbirds. The most numerous species are the American wigeon, northern pintail and mallard. These herbivorous ducks arrive in eelgrass meadows in large numbers beginning in late August and continue to arrive as late as November from breeding grounds in western Canada and Alaska. Wigeons are strictly herbivorous and set upon the leaves of eelgrass, especially the introduced species *Zostera japonica,* whereas the pintail and mallard prefer a more varied diet of seeds and plant stems found in salt marshes and nearby farms.

Another conspicuous species that is dependent on eelgrass is the brant. This sea-going goose eats eelgrass while on the Pacific Coast. Brant return each year to the same eelgrass meadow where they mostly graze the leaves and stems to live through the winter and to fuel their long migration back to the arctic. However, they might also arrive in March to take advantage of herring eggs

The Arctic Connection

In the mid-1980s, Austin Reid, a Canadian Wildlife Service scientist, noticed that the plumage coloration of the bellies of brant on the Pacific Coast resembled the color of breeding grounds across the Canadian Arctic. Since then, banding has confirmed Reid's hunch. Between November and March, most brant in the Strait of Georgia arrive from breeding grounds in western Alaska and the Canadian Arctic. It gets more complicated in Puget Sound. Flocks from northern Puget Sound are largely from colonies in the Canadian High Arctic, with smaller numbers from colonies in Alaska and the Canadian Low Arctic. Olympic Peninsula flocks are mostly from Alaska and the Low Canadian Arctic, whereas flocks in southern Puget Sound are from western Alaska, the Canadian Low Arctic or both. This discovery shows that brant populations in each bay are sustained by colonies from a small part of the Arctic.

deposited on eelgrass and other beaches. Following breeding, about 150,000 brant spend the winter on the Pacific Coast in Baja California. They gather in one of the world's largest eelgrass meadow in Izembek Lagoon at the base of the Aleutian Island chain. From there, they launch a transpacific flight of over 5000 kilometers (3125 miles) to Mexico. The flight is demanding – by the time they settle in Mexico the Brant will have lost about one-third of their weight.

Far less conspicuous than the grazing waterfowl are grazing invertebrates. The chink shell is a widespread and easily found snail in eelgrass meadows of Puget Sound and the Strait of Georgia. It measures about 5 millimeters (1/4 inch) in height. Even more conspicuous than the snail are its tiny yellow egg masses, described by Eugene Kozloff as "little yellow life preservers." Also abundant is one of my favorite denizens of the eelgrass meadows, the bubble snail, whose bulging body can hardly be contained in its dainty shell. It lays its yellow eggs in bands resembling narrow strands of decaying gauze along the leaves of eelgrass. Where the bubble snail is abundant, the tidal wrack becomes littered with its paper-thin shells.

Grazers also find food on the mudflats. A film of greenish algae covering mudflats in spring and summer feeds large numbers of herbivorous horn snails, which were introduced with the Japanese oyster earlier this century.

Grazers in the salt marsh include mice and voles from neighboring grasslands and forest. The most ubiquitous species is the deer mouse, which roams the salt marsh largely at night. It nests under driftwood and below ground. About all you see of the Townsend's vole is a fleeting glimpse as it torpedoes along its runways in the grass and down its burrow. Voles live much of their lives underground but on wet wintry days, a rising water table can force them above ground.

DETRITUS FEEDERS

*Deep down here by the dark water lived Old Gollum, a slimy creature. I
don't know where he came from, nor who or what he was. He was Gollum –
as dark as darkness, except for two big round pale eyes in his thin face.*
– J. R. R. Tolkien, *The Hobbit*

Winter storms tear apart the leaves of eelgrass and batter the dried salt marsh
plants. The dead leaves and stems scatter about the beach and tumble into the
salt marsh to become food for animals that live on plant detritus. Many worms
inhabiting eelgrass meadows and neighboring beaches go unnoticed but play
an important role in converting the detritus into animal protein. If you look
closely at the mud on a warm day, it will appear to be moving. The top few centimeters (a few inches) of some mudflats are crawling with marine worms,
crustaceans and amphipods. Their vulnerability to predators destines them to a
life in the roots and sand away from prying eyes.

Several species of lugworms that live in and around eelgrass meadows are
also abundant in estuaries. An abundant polychaete worm in eelgrass meadows
is *Notomastus tenuis* which lives by eating sediment. One of the most important
group of detritus feeders that live on the substrate beneath the eelgrass canopy
and on neighboring mudflats are the crustaceans, notably the copepods,
amphipods, isopods and shrimps. These little animals are high on the list of
entrees for many fish. Copepods are seldom longer than one millimeter (1/16
inch) but they are very numerous and haute cuisine for gunnels, herring,
salmon and sea perch. They become abundant in spring and early summer
when the water warms. Also important are the amphipods that devour algae
and detritus. The best-known amphipods are the beachhoppers, which leap and
scurry when wave-washed algae is turned aside. The genus *Corophium* contains
several important species that consume detritus from eelgrass, epiphytes,
marine algae and animal remains. They remove food from water by the waving
motions of their abdominal appendages and legs fringed with tiny hairs. Often
more abundant than *Corophium* are tiny mysid shrimp, which race through the
water resembling miniature motorboats.

The ghost shrimp lives a Gollum-like existence in muddy burrows often in
association with eelgrass meadows. It seldom is seen at the surface, but telltale
volcano-shaped burrow entrances belie its presence. A small fish, the arrow

goby, has taken up residency in the burrows of ghost shrimps, along with other shrimps, worms and small crabs.

The smallest of the North American sandpipers, the least sandpiper, is abundant in Pacific salt marshes. It weighs about 20 grams (2/3 ounce). Least sandpipers often accompany migrating western sandpipers, which they closely resemble. Both species stop at salt marshes and mudflats in April and May on their way north to the breeding grounds, and again on their southbound journey from July through October. The least sandpiper eats copepods, small clams, polychaete worms and other invertebrates along the margins of salt marshes and roosts in the salt marsh during high tide. In southern British Columbia individual birds linger for an average of about five days before departing on their southward migration. They share salt marshes with purple shorecrabs that dig burrows into hard mud. Little is known about the habits of this crab in salt marshes, but it likely preys upon invertebrates and scavenges dead animals brought in by the tide.

BURROWING FILTER FEEDERS

So far, we have been looking mostly at creatures on mudflats or in eelgrass beds and salt marshes. It's now time to get dirty! In the oozing, smelly mud below the eelgrass canopy are several species of clams, worms and arthropods that feed on plankton. The most conspicuous clam is the basket cockle, which lies on or near the surface of the beach where its short siphons can extend into the seawater. The bent-nosed clam is often very abundant here too but lies submerged in the ooze. Both species are also found on neighboring sandflats and mudflats.

Whoever named the inconspicuous macoma must have had an odd sense of humor. The bright pink shells attract the eye of even the least observant. This dainty clam seldom grows larger than one centimeter (1/2 inch) across. It lives in muddy situations where it is a component of the diet of several shorebirds including the western sandpiper and dunlin. The geoduck that inhabits gravel beaches and the Pacific gaper lie buried as much as a meter (39 inches) below the surface. They spurt water from their retractable siphons if disturbed during low tides, often to great delight of unsuspecting beach walkers. All of these clams slurp in plankton and expel wastes through siphons.

PREDATORS

Surface Dwellers

Two men look out through the same bars.
One sees the mud, and one the stars.
– Frederick Langbridge, *Cluster of Quiet Thoughts*

The abundance of clams, shrimps, worms and other invertebrates that dwell in the mud attract predatory crabs, ducks, gulls, shorebirds and even some whales. The Dungeness crab is a conspicuous invertebrate scavenger and predator of the animals in the eelgrass meadow. In California, female crabs molt in late summer and mate before the shell hardens. Eggs are brooded until December or January when hatching occurs. The larvae are then carried offshore to mix with other plankton, where they go through several development changes to become swimming "megalopa" in April and May. Between one and two years later, the megalopae molt into juvenile crabs in coastal areas and finally become adults in two to six years. Dungeness crabs seldom stray inshore of the subtidal eelgrass meadows. Female Dungeness crabs gather in nursery areas along the subtidal edge of eelgrass meadows in the southern Fraser River estuary where their densities can reach up to three to four crabs per square meter (10.5 square feet).

Along with the predatory crabs, the rising tide also brings the sunflower star to hunt clams within the eelgrass meadows. (Starfish are more correctly known as sea stars. The sunflower star is one of about 75 species of sea stars [starfish]).

In Puget Sound the chief prey is the butter clam. Watching sea stars is like watching paint dry, with one exception: the sunflower star is the sprinter of the starfishes, visibly scurrying at breakneck speed of about 1.6 meters (5.2 feet) per minute along the bottom in search of prey. Although very slow for us, it is curiously rambunctious for a sea star. Hidden behind the gentle exterior of the sunflower star is a ferocious hunter feared by bivalves and sea cucumbers alike.

Pity the unfortunate clam that falls prey to *Pycnopodia*. The many-rayed star settles over its victim and systematically lifts sand and gravel out of the way. Small clams and urchins are swallowed whole, while larger victims are forced open by applying unrelenting hydrostatic pressure from its many tentacled feet to overcome the adductor muscle of the clam. Once the valves have parted, *Pycnopodia* everts its stomach between the shells and digests the clam alive.

The glaucous-winged gull, California gull and mew gull are abundant predators in eelgrass beds from Washington to Alaska; the western gull predominates in Oregon and California. The glaucous-winged gull eats ghost shrimps, Dungeness crabs, basket cockles, and fish among other items. Shrimp are snatched from their burrows, crabs are caught by turning over eelgrass and sea lettuce, and cockles are broken from their rugged shells by dropping them to the beach from the air.

The seasonal ebb and flow of tides and day length strongly affect the great blue heron's breeding cycle along the Jade Coast. The lengthening days of spring bring warm sunshine onto the eelgrass meadows, stirring the growth of leaves and their epiphytes. This sudden growth spurt provides food and shelter for millions of gunnels, sticklebacks and sculpins waiting in deep water offshore to breed. Their arrival attracts large numbers of herons to eelgrass meadows. Once each female catches enough fish during the low tides to begin to make eggs, she chooses a mate at the colony and the nesting season begins. Herons require about 100 days to lay and incubate eggs, and raise their chicks.[7] Adults and young depart the nesting colonies between June and August to spend the summer and autumn catching fish in eelgrass meadows. By autumn, the days are noticeably shorter, and a chill settles into the eelgrass meadows. Fish that were abundant a few months earlier dwindle in number in the eelgrass meadows, and herons begin to search elsewhere for food.

SWIMMING PREDATORS

Large filter-feeding invertebrates such as clams, mussels and cockles are the mainstay of large numbers of sea ducks in winter. The mild, ice-free climate and high daytime tides allows them to feast on invertebrates in eelgrass meadows and on nearby mudflats throughout the winter. As many as a fifth of the world's sea ducks spend the winter along the Jade Coast. Among the most numerous and widespread diving ducks are the bufflehead, greater scaup, common goldeneye, surf scoter, white-winged scoter, and long-tailed duck. Scaup sometimes rest on shore and feed in shallow water, but the other species seldom come ashore. Bufflehead and goldeneye are usually found in shallow water; scoters and long-tailed ducks feed in the deepest water, sometimes tens of meters (more than 30 feet) in depth. All of these ducks are largely absent from the Pacific coast between March and September, when they breed in western Canada and Alaska.

For many years, I had marveled and wondered about the importance to the lives of birds, fish, marine life and sea mammals of the annual migrations of herring to the Jade Coast. Educator and friend Rod MacVicar pointed out that the herring spawn rivals the Serengeti in the mass of migratory living tissue. About 300 million kilograms (660 million pounds) of wildebeest make the migration across the Serengeti Plain each year. Compare those figures with the 200 million kilograms (440 million pounds) of herring that enter a single coastal spawning beach on the east coast of Vancouver Island.

In the spring of 2002, Rod and I teamed up with filmmaker Rudy Kovanic to record the event. It was a record cold spring day in March when we drove to Baynes Sound on the east coast of Vancouver Island. Snow is unusual here in spring, but a dusting lay on the ground along the shore. Cold gale-force winds were blowing from the southeast ahead of an approaching weather front. We pulled on extra clothes and rain gear, and zipped up our floater coats in preparation for a few cold hours on the water.

Over the whitecaps we could see the occasional sea lion bobbing at the surface in the shallow waters of the Sound. Groups of five to fifteen sea lions were feasting on schools of herring. Overhead, squealing gulls darted between the sea lions to snatch up wounded herring, and eagles swooped in with feet lowered to grasp herring from between the gulls. Along the shore, flocks of dunlins ran hither and yon, picking up herring eggs clinging to seaweed and sticks on a sandy beach. A few bloated eagles and hundreds of gulls stood on shore digesting their meals. We turned the boat into the lee of an island where small parties of cormorants, grebes, scaup, scoters and long-tailed ducks floated on the waves. In a few weeks, their numbers would swell to over 100,000. A similar scene is played out in many places along the Jade Coast when herring arrive, attracting the attention of birds, whales, sea otters, and sea lions. The sudden arrival of herring and the deposition of eggs creates a late-winter burst of energy into a coastal environment that has laid dormant for months. It is celebrated by the animal safari at the feast, and it is also a likely welcome respite for marine life living on the gravel and sand beaches.

Beginning in February in the south and continuing until July in the north, herring swim into the shallows to lay eggs on vegetation and the beach. Eelgrass meadows are favored, though not exclusive, spawning places. Spawning has been recorded for more than 250 kilometers (400 miles) of shoreline in British

Columbia. In Alaska, the eggs form a thick soup along some shores. Each female herring lays from 9000 to 38,000 eggs depending on its age and size. The sticky eggs adhere to eelgrass, kelp, rockweed and rocks in a gelatinous mat. Males release their sperm in the water, creating white clouds in the spawning areas. The eggs hatch in about ten days depending on the sea temperature, but many provide food for marine invertebrates. The contribution of this energy to the marine ecosystem is immense. On the west coast of Vancouver Island, an estimated 16 million turban snails and 9 million leather stars were estimated to eat 1021 tonnes of herring eggs, and a further 235 tonnes of herring eggs were consumed by gray whales.

For several weeks each spring, herring beaches are a cacophony of screaming gulls, barking sea lions and rumbling fishing boats – all pursuing herring. Larval herring begin to feed on invertebrate eggs, copepods and diatoms, and fall prey to jellyfish and small fish. They grow rapidly so that about one month after hatching, young herring are 2.5 to 4 centimeters (1 to 2 inches) long. At this age, copepods remain their principal food but their, diet widens to include barnacle and mollusc larvae, bryozoans, rotifers and small fish. They form into schools for the summer and in the fall move offshore into deeper waters. Herring fatten through the summer and fast in winter, relying on stored oils to fuel the development of eggs and sperm. Large numbers gather to feed at the mouth of the Fraser River estuary in May and June.

Herring are one of the mainstays of many fish, birds and mammals on the Pacific Coast. Herring eggs are consumed during the spawn from late winter to early spring in eelgrass meadows and other intertidal areas, and the fish are consumed year-round while at sea. The amount of spawn varies from year to year, and in good years over 100,000 loons, gulls, and ducks have been counted at one feast. One estimate put the amount of spawn eaten by 75,000 scoters at 103 tonnes. The significance of herring in the lives of many coastal species has not been fully realized. The sudden appearance of this bountiful food supply could very well prepare many birds and marine mammals for breeding and migration. The eggs are also food for snails, crabs and scavenging invertebrates.

Soon after the herring depart, other fish arrive to breed in eelgrass meadows. As part of my doctoral research, I hauled a beach seine net through eelgrass meadows to estimate their seasonal abundance. The nets capture a large number of fish that would go undetected otherwise. We would pull the net ashore

One of the many remarkable natural events on the Jade Coast is the spring spawning by the Pacific herring. Each female herring deposits thousands of eggs that cling to seaweed and rocks. From these tiny jewel-like eggs, young herring will hatch in about two weeks to begin a life at sea.

and quickly empty the catch into buckets of water. The nets writhed with rigid sticklebacks, wiry pipefish, wiggling gunnels, angry sculpins and sleek shiner perch. For many fish, the abundant food and protection from predators provided by eelgrass meadows make them nurseries of choice for their growing young.[8] The abundance of small fish in eelgrass meadows following the arrival of spawning herring might be more than coincidental. Herring spawn might be an important additional source of nutrients for invertebrates that are the prey of small fish in the eelgrass ecosystem.

Meet the Pricklebacks

Pricklebacks, cockscombs, warbonnets, shannies and eelblennies are members of a large, but obscure blenny family of small fish. Most of the fifty-four species live in the north Pacific Ocean where they are on the menu of many large fish, and diving and wading birds. Their eel-like shape allows them to wriggle out of reach of predators in small crevices and under rocks. My favorite – the decorated warbonnet – sports projections on the head and back, and rests on oversized pectoral fins.

The shiner sea perch leave subtidal waters for the shallows of eelgrass meadows in spring to give birth. Female perch carry up to thirty-five young in their distended bellies. Young perch are born largely in June and July. Once they have given birth, females mate with the males sporting black courtship colors for the occasion. The sperm stored in her ovary waits about six months before penetrating the ovary wall and fertilizing the eggs in late autumn. Meanwhile, the recently born young grow quickly in the warm waters, hidden from most predators in the tangle of eelgrass leaves where they remain until their departure for deep water in autumn. Copepods are important in the perch diet early in life, and mussels, marine worms, shrimps, and barnacles are eaten later in life. Herons, eagles, cormorants, kingfishers, mergansers, mink, otters, rockfish, dogfish and salmon eat sea perch.

Lurking among the eelgrass beds and sporting red bellies and spines that lock into position, are the three-spined sticklebacks. Much has been written about stickleback behavior in freshwater, but less is known about the ones that inhabit eelgrass meadows. Sticklebacks are small fish less than 4 centimeters (1.5 inches) from snout to tail. They dine on copepods, amphipods, euphausiids, barnacle and clam larvae, crustaceans, insects and young fish. Sticklebacks are well armed with strong scales along their flanks and sharp spines on their back but this doesn't stop the great blue herons, kingfishers, mergansers and bufflehead from eating large numbers of them.

One of the oddest fishes in eelgrass meadows and a personal favorite is the bay pipefish. Measuring less than half a centimeter (0.4 inch) in depth and up to 33 centimeters (13 inches) in length, the pipefish looks like it has been stretched out of shape. Not only is it odd looking, but it also has an unorthodox breeding behavior. Male pipefish have pouches specially for tending the growing young. Posterior to the anus of the male is a ventral slit, which forms the brood pouch. Sometime in June, males court females by showing off with body shakes and head nodding. An interested female impressed by this show entwines herself around his rigid S-shaped body and transfers the fertilized

Eelgrass meadows are nurseries for a few dozen species of fish. The saddleback gunnel is a numerous species that is eaten by many animals, including herons, cormorants, rockfish and salmon.

eggs into his pouch. He cares for the young until they become independent at about 20 millimeters (16 inches) in length. If this sounds strangely familiar, it is because pipefish are closely related to the sea horses of warmer seas, whose males also tend for the young in special pouches. The bay pipefish has no teeth, so it catches its copepod and amphipod prey by sucking water and prey into its mouth by inflating its cheeks.

Some species of fish use eelgrass meadows as places to grow after hatching in other habitats. One such fish is the gunnel. Gunnels are sometimes mistaken for eels because of the similar body shape. The largest species is the penpoint gunnel. Some monsters reach nearly half a meter (20 inches) in length. The common name refers to a pen nib-like anal spine. Two other abundant species of gunnel are the crescent gunnel and the saddleback gunnel. Both of these species seldom reach 15 centimeters (6 inches) in length. Gunnels are not easily seen because of their cryptic markings. However, they can be caught in large numbers in beach seine nets hauled through eelgrass meadows in spring and summer. They lay eggs in the subtidal in winter and swim into eelgrass meadows in spring to feed on small crustaceans, mollusks and other marine invertebrates. Herons and cormorants eat large numbers of gunnels.

For a better understanding of the magnitude of fish in an eelgrass meadow we can look at some estimates. I roughly estimated that there were about 12,600,000 small fish in 31 hectare (76 acres) of eelgrass meadow on Sidney Island. Now try to imagine how many copepods and amphipods are eaten by 12 million gunnels!

Eelgrass beds are also important nurseries for the English sole, which begins its life as an egg in inshore waters where it hatches to become floating larvae. Young soles are pelagic for six to ten weeks and then move inshore to feed on copepods, barnacle larvae and other small invertebrates. They can be spotted as they scurry from underfoot in a cloudy trail of mud. Adult English soles spend most of their life in subtidal and pelagic waters. English soles are mobile souls that travel along much of the Pacific Coast. The major diet is clams, marine worms, small crustaceans and starfish.

The staghorn sculpin is one of the most noticeable fish in eelgrass meadows. Young sculpins follow the edge of the tide in search of marine worms, clams and other invertebrates, and older, larger individuals lurk in the eelgrass where they eat small crabs, shrimps, fish and invertebrates. Sculpins are an important part of the diet of the merganser, western grebe, kingfisher and river otter. Sculpins and flounders enter eelgrass meadows by following the tides and searching the mudflats for invertebrates in the mud. When the tide is low, invertebrates move down their burrows or bury themselves in the mud, and hordes of shorebirds probe the beaches for them. The common loon frequents the edges of eelgrass meadows where it dives for fish, amphipods, crabs and shrimp. Often in the vicinity of eelgrass beds are flocks of western grebes, especially in Puget Sound and southern Strait of Georgia. Staghorn sculpin, gunnels and shiner sea perch are eaten by these fish eaters.

Completing the survey of swimming predators is the largest species to frequent eelgrass meadows and mudflats – the gray whale. Gray whales eat amphipods, isopods, marine worms, clams and herring eggs. Their habit of sucking up food and expelling mud and sand through the baleen plates leaves telltale pits in the muddy bottom that become pools when the tide ebbs. The gray whale undergoes one of the longest migrations of all mammals. The 9,000 kilometer (14,400 mile) migration along the Pacific coast begins in the breeding grounds in Baja California and ends in the Bering, Chukchi and western Beaufort seas. Over 20,000 whales pass along the coast each spring, reaching peak abundance in March in California, April in British Columbia, and May in Alaska. Some individuals remain along the coasts of California to British Columbia and return with southbound migrants in autumn; others remain year-round. Following a summer of fattening, they return to the lagoons of Mexico to give birth and breed. About a century ago, gray whales were hunted heavily by the whaling industry. Now, with protection, their numbers are increasing, and we are witnessing a slow reoccupation of their former haunts.

AERIAL PREDATORS

Swift as the wind they fly, speeding along the breakers with directness of a runner down a course, and I read fear in their speed – Henry Beston, *The Outermost House, 1928*

Spilling through the frozen Wrangell Mountains onto the coastal lowlands of Alaska is the Stikine River. It begins its life far into the interior of British Columbia's Skeena Mountains. Crossing through some of the wildest territory on the planet, the Stikine slides by the dormant volcano Mount Edziza, scours canyons through the Coast Range and surges to sea through southeast Alaska. At its mouth, the Stikine slows to a meandering pace across a wide pristine delta about 50 kilometers (30 miles) north of the town of Wrangell. Blocks of ice from nearby Le Conte glacier glide by on the silty waters. The Stikine is still a wild place accessible mostly by boat. The sand and mud delta lie largely untouched by humans within the Tongass National Forest. From the air, the Stikine draws in thousands of Central American shorebirds on their migrations to Alaskan breeding grounds. In 1991, we knew very little about how important the Stikine was to shorebirds in the chain of migration mudflats linking the tropics to the Arctic tundra. And so an expedition was mounted.

May 3, 1991 dawned clear and bright when I boarded the plane in Petersburg, to be dropped off at a site where I would rendezvous with Robert Clair from the United States Forest Service and my colleague Terry Sullivan. The plane roared out of Petersburg and swung south past the icy blue floating glaciers calving from Le Conte Glacier. This territory had remained largely

The Stikine River in southeast Alaska is one of a handful of migration hotspots for sandpipers moving north in spring to their tundra breeding grounds.

unchanged since John Muir hiked the canyons of the Stikine in 1879. Wolves and bears lived along the shores, and the meadows of sedge spread out on the flats for many kilometers. The air had spring freshness.

There is something exciting about spending time in the wilderness relying on your survival skills and exploring an area where few scientists have trodden. I could see Robert and Terry in the boat off to the starboard side, and I could hardly wait for the plane to put down so I could get ashore. We slid on the water surface on a soft landing, unloaded the gear into the boat and headed for a small cabin on Little Dry Island.

E E L G R A S S   M E A D O W S   A N D   S A L T   M A R S H

That evening, we rigged up our equipment to detect radio transmitters that I had attached to sandpipers on the Fraser River delta in British Columbia a few days earlier. The receiver hissed through headphones as I began to scroll through the radio frequencies. An ever-so-faint chirp of a radio seemed to peep in the headphones, but I wasn't certain. Quickly I climbed on to a high point and heard the chirping once more, but this time it was loud and clear. On the beach before me was a sandpiper carrying a tiny radio transmitter that I had glued to its feathers nearly 1,000 kilometers (600 miles) away. This confirmed our suspicions that at least one bird on the Fraser also stopped on the Stikine delta. We later detected several other radios on birds from the Fraser over the next few days.

The cerulean blue sky along the seashore that evening was streaked with wisps of smoky gray clouds. To the south, a gray rain was moving toward us. About 100,000 shorebirds were anxious to depart. I could hear it in their rallying calls. The high tide had pushed a large flock close to the marsh edge, and their twittering calls periodically erupted in a din of chirps as flocks rose from the beach. Some flocks began to form into long lines in the air and began to climb higher in the sky. I followed with my binoculars their silhouetted shapes against the reddening sky until the dots became specks and the specks merged with the sky. Their next stop would be the Copper River delta. In my imagination, I flew with them.

We spent a few days catching, weighing and banding sandpipers at Little Dry Island and then decided to divide the team into two groups. Robert and I would move to the north to Mallard Slough while the others remained at Little Dry Island.

It was late afternoon before the tide was high enough to float the boat. Slowly we poled our way into deeper water before starting the motor and speeding off to the northwest. It was important to get to Mallard Slough while the tide was high so we could reach the camp. If we missed the high water, we would be stuck overnight on the mudflat.

The jade green waters sped by as we made our way along the delta and soon Robert slipped the boat into a riverine channel. We crept up the delta to a small cabin overlooking a mudflat alive with thousands of shorebirds. Robert and I decided that we should take advantage of the opportunity to band some of the birds. We thought we would be lucky to catch a few birds, so we hastily

Refueling for Flight

Small sandpipers have the remarkable ability to store large amounts of fat to fuel migratory flights. Some individuals carry fat weighing as much as 50 percent of their lean body weight. It is sobering to think that food derived from the mudflat ecosystem on the Jade Coast fuels flights that will see these birds thousands of kilometers to the north the next day. The source of this fuel is the myriad of tiny invertebrates that constitute the food of shorebirds.

erected three sets of aluminum poles with fine mist nets strung out in a row. If we caught twenty birds, it would have been a good day of banding. On cue, the flock wheeled and collided headlong into our nets. There was not time to waste.

At times like this one hopes for divine intervention but seldom are prayers answered. So we began the task of removing the birds and placing them into large boxes. Our backs were straining, our eyes felt as though they were permanently crossed, and our throats were parched by the time all the birds were free from the nets. Now the tedious job of weighing, banding, measuring and recording was to begin. We placed the birds into large boxes so they could move about. By setting up a system, we were able to band and release all the birds quickly and with no casualties. With the last bird on its way, we fell back on our bedrolls to rest. We were hungry, but dinner would have to wait.

Beaches on the Jade Coast support shorebirds at all times of year. One of the first shorebirds to be encountered on mudflats in winter is the dunlin, a species with a circumpolar distribution. The subspecies present on the Jade Coast, *Calidris alpina pacifica,* breeds in western Alaska. It undergoes a feather molt in late summer and returns to the mudflats in September through to November, often in huge flocks to forage on worms and clams during low tide. It feeds both during the day and night. Worms are pulled from the mud and quickly swallowed.

The abundant small invertebrate decomposers and small filter feeders in mudflats are the chief prey of over fifty species of shorebirds along the Pacific

Coast. The most numerous shorebird in spring and summer is the western sandpiper. Large numbers spend the winter on mudflats in California, but only a few western sandpipers remain in northern regions. The western sandpiper breeds in western Alaska and spends the winter along the southeast Atlantic Coast, around the Gulf of Mexico and along the Pacific Coast from California to Peru. In April, hundreds of thousands migrate north through our mudflats and estuaries. They return on their journey to the south in July through September. Western sandpipers eat many small worms and the amphipod *Corophium* on mudflats and in estuaries.

There is indeed something frantic in the way sandpipers feed along the mudflats. They probe and peck at invertebrates in the mud with knowledge that soon the tide will return to cover their foraging sites. Large flocks of shorebirds busying themselves at finding food leave themselves exposed to the sleek and agile peregrine falcon and merlin, which catch their prey by rapid flight and quick turns that once seen will remain etched in your memory.

I have walked the beaches of the Jade Coast on countless occasions to search for falcons. Often it is the frantic frightful flights of shorebirds that alert me to their presence. The shorebirds spring from the mudflat in a desperate bid to gain a height advantage to an incoming falcon. Peregrines are much more successful in their chases if they can surprise the shorebirds while they have their heads down foraging along a beach. But this day was extraordinary.

It was a mid-summer afternoon when I poled the boat ashore on a small sandy beach in southeast Alaska. I had come to search the beaches for shorebirds that migrated north along this coastline in big numbers but were thought to be scarce in summer. Either they took another route, or they flew at high altitude. Sand and mud beaches are uncommon habitats in southeast Alaska and so I thought that if any shorebirds were around, they should gather in a relatively few locations.

The sun was bright, and the clear water lapped the shore in a steady rhythm. The beach was about one kilometer (0.6 mile) long, and I did not expect to see many shorebirds. The marine chart showed another bay across a narrow forested neck of land that I reached in a few minutes. The shore was a mixture of sand and gravel and, through my binoculars, I could make out a small flock of sandpipers pecking the shore for amphipods. This was the first flock I had seen in several days, so I moved closer to see what they were up to. Suddenly the flock wheeled and rose quickly from the beach as a peregrine streaked into their midst. I had not seen the falcon coming. The shorebirds bunched into a tight flock in the air and hastily departed the beach. I tracked them through my binoculars as they climbed high into the southeast sky and were lost from sight.

The falcon's pursuit sometimes begins high in the air from which a spectacular dive on partly closed wings is launched. The aim of this approach to snatch an unsuspecting shorebird from the ground or as it takes flight. A second approach is to use stealth and speed during low-level pursuits to fly down the prey. The latter approach was used on the flock in Alaska – unsuccessfully I might add.

Few species of bird on the Jade Coast is as handsome as the black-bellied plover. Its plaintive cry "keeer" is a fixture of windy, open mudflats they occupy. In winter, the plover's coloration is a drab brown, black and white that it exchanges for a handsome black under parts in spring and summer. Black-bellied plovers hunt their prey by scanning the surface of the mud until they detect the slight movement of an invertebrate and scamper to catch it. Marine worms are an important prey species of plovers, but they also eat small bivalves. Sometimes gulls will take up the chase when a plover flies off with a large morsel. Studies in Britain have shown that black-bellied plovers defend stretches of beach against other plovers.[9] These territories included drainage channels on mudflats where they spend most of the time foraging. On windy days, channels provided territorial plovers with protection from windy blasts that deterred other plovers from staying on the beach. The winds on the Jade

Coastal Falcons

The peregrine falcon on the Pacific Coast is mostly of the *pealei* race that breeds on sea cliffs and eats seabirds during its breeding season. Peregrines use ocean swells to conceal their approach on swimming seabirds. Slipping along a trough, the swift peregrine can dart over a wave top to catch a swimming seabird before it can dive to safety. The diet of the peregrine outside the breeding season includes shorebirds, waterfowl, gulls and songbirds.

Coast mudflats seldom gust as high as those in some British estuaries, but plovers depart our mudflats on blustery days to eat earthworms and insects or rest in nearby fields.

Where the mud is particularly soft, the short-billed dowitcher and long-billed dowitcher are sometimes numerous. Dowitchers have long bills with sensitive touch receptors in their tips that they use to probe for worms, crustaceans, fish eggs, small snails and clams.

As a rule, prey outnumbers predators. The greatest amount of the sun's energy is held in eelgrass leaves, which becomes food for trillions of invertebrates, which are eaten by thousands of shorebirds, which become prey to a handful of falcons. In the salt marsh, a few rough-legged hawks, common barn owls and northern harriers hunt thousands of mice and voles that nibble at tonnes of vegetation.

The languid marine waters of the eelgrass meadow allow many delicate animals and plants to live out lives in relative serenity. But where the seawater mixes with freshwater emanating from land, animals and plants able to cope with sudden shifts of salinity replace those preferring marine conditions in eelgrass meadows. The waters of estuaries are sometimes rich with nutrients streaming from the land, but special adaptations are required to survive in this changing ecosystem. This is the subject of the next chapter.

The Fraser River estuary in southwestern British Columbia is a great biological treasure on the Jade Coast. Like many of the great rivers on the Jade Coast, it originates in snowy mountains.

CHAPTER 7

Estuaries

Tidal creeks and estuaries and the crooked, meandering arms of many little rivers whose mouths lap at the edge of the ocean cut through sodden land that seems to rise and fall and breathe with the recurrence of the daily tides.

– Paul Gallico, "The Snow Goose," 1940

I am fortunate to have an office located at the mouth of one of the great rivers on the Jade Coast. The Fraser River delta is home to some of the greatest concentrations of fish and birds on the western shore of North America. From my window, I see flocks of snow geese wing overhead, swans trumpet their presence, and eagles pass by to nest a few hundred meters away. In April, I get the first whiff of spring when the scent of early green shoots of sedge is carried ashore on a fair westerly wind.

The great sedge meadows that form at the mouth of large rivers of the Pacific are desolate places when the tide is at its low ebb. The wind sighs through them and the pungent scent of sedge and mud are in the air. But with the rising tide, life begins to stir in the mud. A sense of urgency fills the air when millions of shorebirds scurry ahead of the rising tide in search of worms to gather the energy for evening flights that will carry them to Alaska. Salmon ride the rising floodwaters to ease their journey against the outflow of the river.

Estuaries are among the greatest biological factories on Earth. Where rivers and streams enter the sea, the diluted seawater creates an environment with immense numbers of fish, birds and invertebrates. There are six major estuaries in northern California, eighteen in Oregon, thirty or so in Washington, over 400 in British Columbia, and several hundred in southeast Alaska. Jade Coast estuaries support a staggering abundance of individuals but a scant few indigenous species. The Fraser River estuary holds hundreds of thousands, sometimes millions, of birds on a single day, and over 20 million salmon can pass through it in a few weeks. But none of these animals live out their entire lives there – they are visitors on their way to breeding sites on distant shores. Unlike Atlantic and Gulf Coast estuaries that have many unique species of animals, there are few true Pacific estuarine fish, no strictly estuarine crabs, and no large prawns or oysters. Why is such a nutrient-rich environment not home to a host of resident species? To answer this question requires an understanding of the workings of the estuary environment.

The Nuts and Bolts of Estuarine Environments

Estuaries are harsh environments bathed in nutrients. The ceaseless ocean tides, flowing nutrients, fluctuating temperature and oxygen levels, and the shifting substrate are more than most plants and animals can cope with throughout their lives. Those plants and animals that do live in estuaries must deal with searing heat in summer, drifting mud and sand, and sudden changes in water temperature. Bound by the cool mud, soft-bodied burrowing invertebrates duck the daytime heat at the mud surface in summer or chilling cold of winter. Even the warm seawater carried ashore by the tides takes time to penetrate the ooze. For organisms living in the mud, cool temperatures alter their ability to grow and reproduce, and the sediments swept up by ocean currents expose them to predators or clog their breathing apparatus. For plants and animals living on rocky or gravel shores, the problems are very different. There are many places that provide a foothold but there are few places to hide from the elements or predators. As a result, specialized defenses such as strong attachments and armored shells and spines are commonplace among animals in rocky estuaries.

SALINITY – THE GREAT EQUALIZER

Within the mouth of the river, I was interested by observing how slowly the waters of the sea and river mixed. The latter, muddy and discoloured, from its less specific gravity, floated on the surface of the saltwater. This was curiously exhibited in the wake of the vessel, where a line of blue water was seen mingling in little eddies, with the adjoining fluid. – Charles Darwin, *The Voyage of the Beagle 1845*

One of the most important factors that dictate whether an animal is present or absent in an estuary begins high in the coastal mountains of the Pacific rainforest. The amount of salt in the water determines the ratio of fresh- to seawater in an estuary. Low-elevation headwaters fill their rivers with water in autumn and winter in tandem with the seasonal rainfall, and for most of the year the saltwater from the ocean dominates the estuaries. In contrast, large rivers that have their origins in the high mountains fill with the autumn and winter rains and again in late spring when the snowfields melt. These estuaries are dominated by freshwater for most of the year. Thus, headwater elevation can have a profound impact on the presence and absence of animals in an estuary. The Fraser, Columbia, Stikine and Skeena rivers have predominantly freshwater estuaries whereas the Cowichan, Nanaimo, Nisqually, Courtenay, Campbell, Salmon and Nimpkish rivers and all small creeks have ocean-dominated estuaries.

Oceanographers define salinity as the total weight of salts dissolved in 1 kilogram (2.2 pounds) of water at a sea temperature of 15 degrees Celsius (59 degrees Fahrenheit). The salinity of seawater in the open Pacific Ocean is about thirty-three parts per thousand. We can taste salt in water when the salinity reaches about one part salt in one thousand parts of water. Salinity fluctuations depend on the amount of freshwater entering the estuary from the river and the amount of seawater arriving on the tides. For example, the salinity in the Squamish River estuary changes from about twenty-seven parts per thousand in winter to below four parts per thousand in spring.[1] The few species of fish that can tolerate such large changes in salinity include the three-spined stickleback and staghorn sculpin, and consequently they are often abundant.

Plants and animals in estuaries must also cope with the swings in salinity. Freshwater spewing from rivers and creeks is not as dense as the seawater lying offshore. When runoff is great, the fresh river water glides over the denser seawater for many kilometers. The freshwater layer flowing from the Fraser River is sometimes visible to ferry-goers traveling across the Georgia Strait 20 kilometers (12 miles) to the southeast of the river mouth. The freshwater spewing out to sea allows denser seawater to creep into the estuary along the river bottom, carrying nutrients deep into the estuary. This so-called "salt wedge" of seawater can penetrate several kilometers upstream along the river bottom, immersing freshwater organisms in salty seawater.

For many species of invertebrates, the salinity of the water does not preclude them from entering and proliferating in estuaries. Instead, it is the amount of time they have available to feed and respire that is important. For example, the lugworm digs U-shaped burrows in the mudflats of estuaries. As the tide falls, freshwater from the river spews across the mudflat and the worms retreat into their burrows. Within the relative safety of its saline burrows, the lugworm awaits the rising tide. Its physiological demands will determine how long it can wait before it needs to feed and replenish its oxygen supply. A lugworm can make these adjustments in at least two ways. First, it can burrow at a position on the beach that is exposed and covered by saline water that best matches its physiological needs. Second, it can time its period of inactivity to closely coincide with tidal cycles.[2]

Also determining which plants and animals will be present in estuaries is the interaction of tide and the lay of the land. The distance between the highest and lowest tides is many kilometers in estuaries with wide, flat deltas, but only a few meters are uncovered by tides where streams tumble down vertical cliffs. Low, flat deltas drain more slowly and are covered by slow-moving water for longer periods than steep beaches. As a result, the lay of the land affects the salinity of the estuary and the plants and animals that can live there.

TEMPERATURE, NUTRIENTS, AND OXYGEN

The temperature of river water, seawater, air and exposed intertidal areas can vary many degrees in a day and between seasons. The ocean temperature fluctuates about 14 degrees Celsius (58 degrees Fahrenheit) over a year near our estuaries. River water, on the other hand, can vary as much as 25 degrees Celsius (80 degrees F) in the year. In addition, the tidal flats absorb the heat of the sun warming the incoming tide. Experienced swimmers on the Pacific Coast who know this phenomenon plan their swim once the flood tide has covered beaches exposed to the sun all day.

Estuaries recycle and trap nutrients that provide the building blocks for plant and animal life. Nutrients such as nitrogen and phosphorus adhere to fine sediment particles suspended in the water, which are carried back into the estuary by tides and currents, where they eventually settle.[3] Our large rivers are milky colored because of sediments they carry from the interior. The amount of sediment settling in an estuary depends largely on the source of the river, the amount of outflow and the tidal change. In large rivers, the amount of sediment carried each year boggles the mind. The Fraser River drains over 200,000 square kilometres (77,220 square miles) of terrain and deposits 13 million cubic meters (459 million cubic feet) of sediment per year – equivalent to a one meter (39 inch) by one meter strip of sediment stretching from Vancouver to London, England. Sediment deposits over 230 meters (750 feet) deep have been dropped in places over the 9,000-year history of the Fraser. The Columbia River carries an estimated 420,000 metric tonnes (413,364 tons) of sediment to sea each year, where the ocean currents have swept it into deep water. Sediments from the Columbia are over 35 meters (114 feet) deep 10 kilometres (6.2 miles) northwest of the mouth. In rivers with weaker water currents, the deposition occurs closer to the river mouth. Heavier sand particles drop along the river's edge and near the outer edge of the estuary. Finer mud deposits where the current is weak such as in bays, sloughs, and on wide tidal flats. Fine particles retain more water, reduce the circulation of water, and consequently have lower levels of dissolved oxygen.

Animals living in mud seldom have to cope with a shortage of water, but they must be able to cope with low oxygen.[4] Estuarine waters in the Pacific Northwest are usually saturated with oxygen but some estuaries, such as Grays Harbor and Coos Bay, suffer from a shortage of oxygen in summer. Some invertebrates overcome the oxygen shortage through anaerobic respiration, a physiological short-term solution to oxygen debt. Animals breathe oxygen and exhale carbon dioxide, but when the body demands more oxygen than it can receive, anaerobic respiration takes over (A by-product of anaerobic respiration is lactic acid that we experience following a day of exercise of overworked muscles).

The organic soup on mudflats allows anaerobic microbes to flourish in the anoxic layer just below the surface of the mud. This layer is readily recognized by a black layer that reeks of hydrogen sulphide, a metabolic waste product of bacteria that live in the mud. These bacteria use hydrogen sulphide during photosynthesis, which creates a "rotten egg" smell. Below this black layer there is little or no oxygen. Animals that make mudflats their home live on its surface, bury themselves in the mud or live in burrows where they can shuttle to and fro between the aerobic and anaerobic environments. Snails crawl over the mud surface, never penetrating more than the top few millimetres of mud. Clams bury deep in mud, often in the oxygen-poor layer, and push their siphons out of the mud to breathe, feed and discharge wastes. The polychaete worms tunnel through the mud or live in tubes made from mud and proteinaceous glue. Few echinoderms can tolerate the conditions of muddy estuaries so starfish, sea cucumbers and sea urchins that are abundant elsewhere on the Jade Coast are rare and ecologically unimportant on estuarine deltas.

Estuarine Food Webs

The lives of plants and animals able to withstand the fluctuating environmental conditions are interconnected in many complex ways. One important connection is their relationships as food. There are essentially three major food webs in estuaries. One web connects phytoplankton, plankton feeders and predators. A second food web connects marsh plants to grazing animals, and a third web links the detritus from these plants to scavenging animals and their predators. All estuaries have components of these three food webs in different amounts depending largely on the estuarine environment. Phytoplankton and marine algae fuel small estuaries dominated by seawater, whereas the large, freshwater-dominated estuaries are predominantly marsh plant- and detritus-based ecosystems.

The producers inhabiting small estuaries are phytoplankton, marine algae and salt marsh plants. The grazers include animals, such as marine snails, that eat algae, and consumers of marsh plants, such as some ducks. The filter feeders are mostly molluscs like mussels, clams and barnacles. The predators are ducks, crabs, and fish that eat molluscs.

The producers that inhabit large estuaries are mostly marsh plants such as Lyngby's sedge and rushes; grazers include the snow goose and muskrat. However, most animals in large estuaries derive their food from the breakdown of detritus – the decay of marsh plants. This food pathway includes detritus feeders such as bacteria, filter feeders such as clams, and predators such as crabs, fish, birds, and a few mammals.

THE PRODUCERS: ESTUARY PLANTS

But sometimes, with sunrise and sunset, sky and land are aflame with red and golden fire. – Paul Gallico, "The Snow Goose," 1940

Sedges and rushes that prefer brackish conditions[5] predominantly clothe estuarine marshes in the mouths of large rivers. Marsh plants occur in bands depending on their particular tolerances to salinity and exposure to water and air. The deepwater marsh consists of common three-square bullrush and sea bulrush, which remain submerged about half the time. The upper marsh is covered mostly by Lyngby's sedge, which is submerged for less than 5 percent of the time. In the shallowest marsh are two freshwater species common to interior wetlands: the cattail and tule. Also tucked in the upper edges of the marsh is the Pacific silverweed. In the more marine estuaries, the upper beach is often inhabited with salt-tolerant species such as wild rye, saltgrass, glasswort and other species typically found in salt marshes. Rockweeds are commonly found clinging to rocks farther down the beach, and filamentous green algae coats the rocks in streams. Sheets of sea lettuce will grow on soft sediments in marine-dominated estuaries. A trained naturalist can deduce the salinity gradient within an estuary by looking at the distribution of its marsh plants.

The marsh plants' rate of growth is governed by the amount of sunlight and nutrients they receive and the temperature and salinity of the surrounding water. Some researchers have estimated for the deepwater marsh a range as great as 550 to 1000 grams (17 to 32 ounces) of plant biomass per square meter (10.7 square feet) of marsh.[5] The Fraser River marshes grow about 2.5 times as much green matter as a comparable area of the best farmland in the Pacific Northwest. Microscopic algae also need stable mudflats where they will not be washed out to sea or covered by wave-washed sediments.

GRAZERS

Many of the grazers in small estuaries are animals typically found on intertidal areas outside the estuary, so the food web closely resembles that of rocky shores and calm bays and beaches. Details of the rocky shore ecosystem are provided in Chapter 4, but a few animals found in small estuaries are worthy of our attention, if for no other reason to illustrate their adaptability to many habitats.

The periwinkles and limpets found along much of the Jade Coast also occur in estuaries, where they scour rocks clean of algae with a rasping radula – a mouthpart covered in small teeth. New teeth in a conveyor-belt process replace wear on the radula. These small snails are often abundant, sometimes exceedingly so. They possess a lung that allows them to live much of the time out of

Farms and Ducks

Christmas bird counts across North America showed that the Puget Sound and Fraser River estuaries support some of the highest densities of American wigeon on the continent.[6] Herbivorous ducks digest far less of the food energy from grass as omnivorous ducks do from their varied diet. Thus, the wigeon have to spend more of the day foraging, and as a consequence were more sensitive to disturbance and less widespread as omnivorous species such as the mallard.

water near the splash zone. The American wigeon and Canada goose also often inhabit small and large estuaries. Like the periwinkles, the wigeon and geese graze on algae, especially sea lettuce, eelgrass and lawns.

Similar to the small, marine-dominated estuary, the grazing food web in freshwater-dominated estuaries is short. However, rivers with freshwater-dominated estuaries have a large flow of water that carries large quantities of sediment and often have wide deltas with extensive marshes. The marshes support many species not found in abundance in other coastal habitats. For example, many ducks commonly found in upland marshes and freshwater-dominated estuaries are much scarcer elsewhere along the seashore.

A few species of birds have the digestive enzymes to consume food energy contained in the stems, leaves, roots

The New Kids on the Block

Numerous species have been accidentally or purposefully added to Pacific estuaries. Over 200 introduced species have been identified in San Francisco Bay and 100 in estuaries in Oregon. The new immigrants include the soft-shelled clam, varnish clam, Japanese oyster, Japanese littleneck clam, screw shell, mute swan, European green crab, and cordgrass. At least twenty-seven species of Japanese and Atlantic coast molluscs were freeloaders of the oyster industry.

Although it is too early to know the impact of introduced species in Pacific estuaries, we should heed the impact one species had on the Atlantic coast. The periwinkle colonized the Atlantic coast from Nova Scotia to New Jersey between 1860 and 1890 and resulted in a change in the number of species, the abundance and the distribution of animals and plants on Atlantic shorelines.[7]

and seeds of marsh plants. There are also a few insects and mammals in Pacific estuaries that are herbivorous. The seeds of brackish marsh plants form one of the most important components in the diet of mallards, northern pintails, American wigeon and green-winged teal in these estuaries.[8] Seed production is partly dependent on the salinity of the water; sedges in more saline areas produce only a fraction of the seeds of sedges in brackish habitats. It is estimated that between 13,000 and 41,000 seeds are produced per square meter (10.5 square feet) of sedge in the Fraser River delta. Herbivorous ducks such as the American wigeon, northern pintail and mallard are abundant in brackish estuaries, especially near farmlands. They are particularly abundant in northern

The estuaries along the Jade Coast harbor many ducks from autumn to spring. One of the most widespread species is the snow goose that spends the autumn and winter digging plant roots and nibbling at grasses.

California, Puget Sound and the southern Strait of Georgia. In the Fraser River delta, about 200,000 of these ducks spend the winter eating seeds, eelgrass and marsh plants in autumn, and discarded and winter-hardy farm crops in winter.[8]

Sedges and bulrushes rhizomes are the principal source of food for the snow goose in estuaries of the Jade Coast. Over 50,000 geese reside in the Skagit and Fraser River estuaries from October to April. Winter tides and storms remove the aboveground plant material, and the geese grub in the marsh muds for the underground roots, known as "rhizomes," which store food reserves for sprouting leaves the following spring. Trumpeter swans also feed on rhizomes and create large craters in the marshes in the process, where herons and shorebirds forage.

Among the many grazers in estuaries are small herbivorous mammals that can sometimes be very numerous although are seldom seen. The Townsend's vole is an abundant meadow mouse that inhabits the upper edges of the estuary where grasslands meet the marsh edge. When the November rains arrive, the rising water table forces the voles from their burrows where they fall prey to northern harriers, rough-legged hawks and great blue herons. In this case, the food chain is only three steps long: plants–voles–hawks.

The muskrat and American beaver are freshwater species that will inhabit brackish portions of the estuary. The muskrat eats mostly roots and stems of marsh plants, and the beaver consumes marsh plants, and bark, leaves and branches of trees.

DETRITUS FEEDERS

Next up are the very important detritus eaters. The vegetation not eaten by grazers eventually dies and disintegrates by the action of waves and scouring sediments to become small particles known as detritus. The resulting particles mix with detritus from forest litter and animal feces to form the basis of the most important food web in freshwater-dominated estuaries. An estimated 90 percent of the food energy originates with the detritus. These microscopic bits of plant material begin to gather together when they enter the turbulent mixing of fresh and saltwater or in silt-laden water of the estuaries to make a kind of biological soup rich in food. By itself, detritus is of no value to most animals; first bacteria, fungi and protozoa must attack detritus. This critical stage in the food web makes detritus digestible to other animals farther along the food web. Fresh detritus from eelgrass is estimated to hold 100,000 bacteria cells per square millimetre.

BURROWING FILTER FEEDERS

The biological soup of plankton and detritus found in estuaries becomes food for filter-feeding invertebrates buried in the sediments, clinging to rocks and swimming in the water. The numbers of species is legion, and space is insufficient to discuss all of them. However, a brief introduction to some of the most important and conspicuous species will provide a snippet of the richness of biological variety that inhabits our estuaries.[9]

Filter feeders derive their food from the surrounding water. A host of organisms get their food in this manner, and many are familiar to us from rocky shores. In small, marine-dominated estuaries, littleneck clams are often present in sandy gravel, but the most estuarine of clams is the soft-shelled clam. This species can tolerate the reduced salinity of estuaries particularly well, and often the beaches are strewn with its thin shells. The soft-shelled clam feeds on particles on the surface of the flooded estuary by extending a siphon as much as 20 centimetres (16 inches) from its seafloor burrow.

Keystone Species

A species whose presence in an ecosystem has profound affects on the presence of other species is known as a keystone species.[10] Recent studies show that the feeding activity of swans and geese in the Fraser River estuary are having a profound affect on the marsh. The swans and geese consume about 30 to 40 percent of the rhizomes in the marsh each year, and their method of digging allows erosion to remove a few centimeters (a few inches) from the surface each year.[11] Most ecologists have dismissed birds as being of minor importance in the ecological functions of estuaries. This view should be re-evaluated considering that marsh plants are the source of much of the energy that enters the estuarine detritus cycle.

The Vital Role of the Humble Bacterium

Most animals require food with an average carbon to nitrogen ratio of less than seventeen to avoid protein deficiency. Decomposers reduce the carbon-nitrogen ratio in detritus by producing proteins and carbohydrates. The rate at which bacteria can convert detritus into the size and nutritional condition usable by other animals is one of the most important ecological features determining the number of animals farther along the food web.[12]

Clams

The soft-shell clam was introduced to the Pacific Coast with transplants of oysters to San Francisco Bay in 1869. It is now one of the most abundant clams along the coast. The success of this species in estuaries is likely due to its ability to survive in oxygen-free environments for many days. This feature is not uncommon among bacteria but is a physiological revolution among molluscs.

In contrast to the small estuaries, large estuaries often have muddy deltas. Living in these large muddy sediments are several invertebrates that are difficult to see without the aid of a microscope. These include a variety of tiny benthic invertebrates and diatoms that are important sources of food for estuarine animals. Some species vacuum the estuary floor, others gobble or nibble at detritus bits, many filter food from the water, and some eat each other. Of the animals that are visible to the naked eye, the worms, clams and their relatives, and crustaceans are most conspicuous. However, they are not readily apparent without digging into the mud.

One animal that leaves a telltale sign of its presence is the bamboo worm; it forms tiny tubes that jut a few centimeters above the mud, often in great numbers. Also conspicuous in muddy situations often quite high on the beach is a lugworm; it leaves coiled fecal castings outside its L- or J-shaped burrow. Lugworms are found in muddy habitats in both the Pacific and Atlantic Coasts where they eat detritus. Other conspicuous worms can occur by the hundreds in a few square centimeters (few square inches) of mud. Also present in muddy situations are Macoma clams, a tiny snail called the chink shell, ostracods, and the crustaceans *Corophium* and *Tanais,* as well as tiny green shorecrabs.

SURFACE DWELLERS

Especially abundant beneath rocks and boulders of marine-dominated estuaries is the green shorecrab. This small crab is part of the beach cleanup crew that doubles as a predator of mussels and other invertebrates. It prefers beaches with freshwater drainage and therefore is more likely to be found in estuaries than its close relative, the purple shorecrab. Both species dine on dead animals that settle on the bottom.

Far more retiring than the green shorecrab are the surface-dwelling zooplankton. Rotifers, cladocerans, ostracods, calanoids, harpatacoids, cyclops, mysids, cumacids, amphipods and isopods – hardly a lineup of household names – these tiny creatures are the food of molluscs, crustaceans, fish and other animals. One researcher estimated up to 670,000 of these animals inhabited a cubic meter (35.3 cubic feet) of mud!

On the mud surface or just below it are molluscs and crustaceans that eat mostly zooplankton and detritus. The bent-nosed clam is often the most conspicuous mollusc, although shells from dead individuals are more evident than live specimens. It is an adaptable species that can live in very sour water of undrained estuaries as well as in eelgrass beds. It feeds through extended siphons that vacuum the mud surface of sediments. Also feeding on detritus in mud sediments are tiny amphipods, *Corophium*, that seldom exceed 1 centimetre (2.4 inches) in length. These amphipods can number in the hundreds in a few square centimeters (few square inches) of mud and are a major source of food for birds and fish. The western sandpiper, least sandpiper, green-winged teal, staghorn sculpin, juvenile salmon and many other animals eat amphipods.

Where estuarine worms, crustaceans and molluscs are abundant there are often shorebirds such as sandpipers, plovers, dowitchers and so on. The Jade Coast mudflats attract about fifty species of shorebird each year. Shorebirds catch their prey using touch-sensitive bill tips that probe deep into the mud, by probing near the surface, or by picking invertebrates off the mud. The killdeer, the most widespread shorebird in North America, is as at home on mudflats as it is in farmlands. It often advertises its presence by loud calling of its namesake "killdeer-killdeer." The diet of the killdeer includes insects and intertidal invertebrates. The latter are sometimes caught by rapidly stirring the mud with the foot, presumably to lull invertebrates into moving. The spotted sandpiper is

The glaucous-winged gull patrols estuarine beaches in search of worms, clams, crabs and fish that they eat or export to their young waiting in nesting colonies on nearby islands.

139

Seawater Receptors

Mussels have sensory receptors near their siphons to detect changes in salinity. When the salinity gets too low for its liking, the mussel clamps its valves shut and awaits the return of saltier water. The process occurs in three stages, beginning when salinity drops to twenty-six parts per thousand and ending with tightly closed shells when salinity drops to about twenty parts per thousand. Tiny amounts of water that seep between the shells of the mussel signal when conditions are suitable to open. Barnacles behave similarly to mussels by closing when the salinity drops and opening when saline conditions return.

also ubiquitous along stream edges and in estuaries with muddy deltas. The dunlin is widespread in large Jade Coast estuaries. Flocks of several thousand are not uncommon on large muddy beaches. They wheel across beaches creating helioscopic views of their white undersides and duff-colored backs. Often associated with dunlin but in far fewer numbers is the black-bellied plover. In April and May, and later from July through September, migrating western sandpipers and least sandpipers join the plovers on our muddy estuaries.

Four common species of gull that frequent estuarine mudflats are the glaucous-winged gull, California gull, mew gull and ring-billed gull. All four species scavenge dead fish, birds, invertebrates and human refuse. The glaucous-winged gull resides in the winter along the entire Jade Coast and breeds from Washington to Alaska. California and ring-billed gulls breed on the prairies of Canada and the United States. They migrate westward to the Jade Coast, arriving in July through October, before flying south for the winter to California and Central America. California gulls are also numerous in offshore waters. Mew gulls breed mostly in Alaska and feed along a variety of shores. The ring-billed gull is mostly found in farmlands and estuarine habitats while on the Pacific coast. It eats flying insects, termites and earthworms caught in farmlands, and invertebrates and small fish on beaches.

Feeding on suspended sediments in the water above the mud are a few species of molluscs. The butter clam, bay mussel and several species of barnacle grow larger outside estuaries, where water salinity is more constant, but both can survive the changing salinity of an estuary. Mussels and clams filter food particles by pumping seawater through their siphons, whereas barnacles catch food in net-like appendages swept through the water. These invertebrates become food for the purple star, diving ducks such as the white-winged scoter and surf scoter, and the glaucous-winged gull. A conspicuous mollusc that lives on the surface of estuarine beaches is the Japanese oyster, which has done well in only a small number of sites where water temperatures are sufficiently warm to allow spawning. Its thick shell provides protection from most predators.

Several species of snails live on the surface of mudflats where they graze on microalgae. These include an introduced species, the screw shell, and the two species of periwinkle. Screw shells are more numerous in quiet bays, while the periwinkles are more numerous in the rocky shore, but both occur in the more saline estuaries. The periwinkles are one of the first species to be encountered on the shore since they prefer to live high on the beach. Screw shells are found at about the 3-meter (10-foot) tideline.

The Dungeness crab and its smaller relative, the red rock crab, can tolerate small changes in salinity and is sometimes found in estuaries. Both species are more abundant in eelgrass ecosystems, and the red rock crab also lives in rocky habitats. These crabs scavenge dead animals and prey upon molluscs by cracking the shells with heavy pincers.

SWIMMING PREDATORS

Each turn of the tide brings a suite of swimming predators into the estuary. These predators are some of the most familiar animals, including many fish, birds and mammals. However, the water of estuaries also teems with tiny zooplankton that feed on suspended particles and prey on one another. To see these miniature animals requires the aid of a microscope and their role in the ecology of estuaries is not well known. The most numerous zooplankton are *Pseudocalanus*, *Corycaeus anglicus* and *Acartia*.

Several species of shrimp live along the bottom of estuaries or in its waters. An abundant species in our estuaries is the crangoid shrimp, especially the bay crangon. It occurs in intertidal areas and seems to tolerate low salinities of estuaries. In Yaquina Bay, Oregon, the females are present from December to the middle of August. The larger females spawn earlier than smaller individuals, so that hatching occurs in two waves. Shrimps eat detritus and invertebrates and fall prey to birds, fish and whales.

One of the most ubiquitous species of fish in Pacific estuaries is the Pacific staghorn sculpin, also known as the bullhead because of its large head and horn-like spines. The species name armatus refers to three preopercular spines on either side of the head. Sculpins dart away in a cloud of silt when frightened near the shore, and when caught a disgruntled sculpin shows its displeasure by flaring the gill covers and erecting spines on the gills and back. Staghorn sculpins are present in estuaries year-round, but are most numerous from late winter until August. They tolerate a range of salinity, from seawater to nearly freshwater. Spawning occurs mostly in February, and larvae are present from August until March. Sculpins grow to a length of about 14 centimeters (6 inches) in the first year. These small fish are voracious eaters. Their large mouths and small tails make them look like tapered bags with fins. Most of their food is caught on or near the surface of the mud. Invertebrates and small fish are caught following the tide, sometimes resulting in strandings during ebbing tides.

Their habit of feeding in shallow water means that sculpins often fall prey to fish-eating birds, including the great blue heron, hooded merganser, and double-crested cormorant. These birds also eat flounders, especially the small speckled sanddab, which shares the mudflat surface with the sculpin where it hides partly buried in the muddy bottom. Sanddabs grow to about 14 centimetres (6 inches) long and spawn in Puget Sound around February. They hunt largely by ambushing their prey from the seclusion of the mud.

Several species of diving ducks depend on the presence of clams, snails and shrimps as food to get them through winter in Jade Coast estuaries. The widespread bufflehead usually feeds alone or in small groups with the common goldeneye. The surf scoter is often seen in estuaries in flocks numbering in the hundreds and occasionally in the thousands. The bufflehead and goldeneye usually feed closer to shore than the scoter. The greater scaup feeds in very shallow water and often roosts on beaches.

Venturing into estuaries are a few insects typically found in freshwater habitats. The water strider skims along the surface searching for insects downed on the water. On the streambed, caddisflies spend their immature stages in a home

fashioned from bits of leaves, twigs and stream debris. Winged adults emerge in summer to disperse their eggs to new streams.

Caddisflies are important food for cutthroat trout and young salmon, which lurk in pools along the streams. The cutthroat trout is among our most handsome of fishes. Its spotted, dark-green back blends into olivaceous flanks and silver underbelly. A pink sheen highlights its gill covers, and a yellow or most

In streams, just above the tide where pools of water form is the home to insects such as the water strider and caddisfly. Both are food to cutthroat trout waiting in the shadowy corners of ponds. Angus Creek, British Columbia.

143

The Eulachon

In the last century, eulachons were an important part of the economy between native coastal people bartering with interior peoples. The oil from this fish is unusual in that it remains solid at normal temperatures, allowing easy transport. Adults enter the rivers to spawn in sandy bottoms. Their tiny eggs have two membranes; the outer membrane ruptures when the egg is deposited on the river bottom, quickly exposing a sticky surface to sand grains. About one month later, depending on water temperature, the eggs hatch into larvae about 5 millimeters (0.2 inches) long that are carried away to sea by river and ocean currents. The death of many adult eulachon following spawning attracts predators into estuaries such as mew gulls, Steller sealions and harbor seals.

often red slash in skin folds of the lower jaw give its name. Cutthroats are predators of insects, worms, fish eggs, frogs and small fish. They live in parts of rivers and estuaries where the water gathers in pools. A quiet observer will sometimes be rewarded with a glimpse of this beautiful creature darting for a floating morsel. Most cutthroats are less than 40 centimetres (15.7 inches) long. Cutthroats spawn in May in the gravel of clear streams. An average female lays about 1,000 eggs that hatch six to seven weeks later. Most young cutthroat remain in their streams until they are two to three years old. Then some coastal populations leave for the sea in spring and summer where they remain for most of a year.

Other fish in the estuaries are mostly marine species that enter rivers to spawn. From the sea, a smelt known as the eulachon, oolichan and candlefish enters large rivers such as the Fraser, Nass, and Skeena in British Columbia, and the Unik, Stikine, Taku, Chilkat and Kenai in Alaska to spawn in March, April or May. Its arrival is heralded by hordes of sealions, and birds gather to feast on the schools of fish. Many eulachons die after spawning, and their larvae return to the sea. Eulachon larvae eat copepods, phytoplankton, mysids, barnacle and worm larvae, and each other. Juvenile and adult eulachons dine on copepods and euphausiids.

A strictly marine species that penetrates the outer edge of estuaries is the Pacific herring. It is very abundant in the plume of the Fraser River in May and June, where it eats ostracods, copepods, fish larvae, and diatoms. Larger young eat mainly crustaceans. As adults, they spawn in shallow marine waters.

Less conspicuous than the eulachon but more widespread in estuaries and rivers along the coast is the three-spined stickleback. The stickleback is one of the most adaptable fish species on the Jade Coast. Besides estuaries, it is found in eelgrass beds, pelagic waters and freshwater. There is some doubt about whether it can reproduce in seawater, but in estuaries and rivers, the male stickleback builds a nest of vegetation in which a female will lay her eggs following an appropriate show of colors and courtship dance by her suitor. The male then guards the eggs and young until the nest is vacated. Nothing is known about their diet in estuaries, but in freshwater habitats sticklebacks eat mostly insects. Many fishes found mostly in marine habitats venture into estuaries.[13] The shiner sea perch, bay pipefish and blennies are a few examples.

Double-crested cormorants, great blue herons, common mergansers and red-breasted mergansers are among the most abundant fish-eating birds in Jade Coast estuaries. Double-crested cormorants are year-round residents of soft-bottomed estuaries in southern British Columbia, Washington, Oregon and California. They nest on isolated islands and on bridge supports, river pilings and other human-built structures. Cormorants are diving birds that swim after their prey. Herons forage in estuaries throughout the year, where they catch sea perch, gunnels, sticklebacks, flatfish and sculpins.

Mammals are also present on mudflats in Jade Coast estuaries. The harbor seal is an abundant mammal and an important predator of fish. It is also at home along much of the coastline and in the major rivers. Scores of harbor seals haul out on icebergs at the toe of glacial estuaries. About 285,000 harbor seals live along the north Pacific from Baja California to Alaska. In estuaries, seals eat fish, especially eulachon, and also sculpins, salmon and flounders.

Fish-Eating Birds

Estuaries have an exceptionally diverse number of fish-eating birds that catch their prey in very different ways. Loons, grebes, cormorants, murrelets and mergansers dive from the water surface for fish. Herons wade in shallow water for their prey. Gulls feed from the surface or make shallow dives from the air. Terns and kingfishers plunge from the air, and eagles snatch fish near the surface of the water. A group of squabbling gulls on the water surface often signals that fish have been driven from the depths by diving birds or predatory fish.

The Salmon

Chinook salmon and coho salmon have been closely studied in the Fraser River estuary. Fry and smolts of both species are most abundant in the estuary from March to August. Within that period there are juvenile chinook that conform to three general patterns of freshwater occupancy. Chinook fry that emerge from eggs laid in autumn remain in the Fraser River and its estuary for short periods, with peak abundance in mid-April. A second group of fry remain in freshwater for two to five months before migrating to sea as smolts in August. The third group of chinook are stream-type fry that remain in freshwater for a year before migrating to sea as smolts. This group derives from eggs laid far upstream from the estuary and pass through the estuary between March and June.[13]

Mudflats provide pupping sites for females. Pups are born in June in northern Puget Sound and the Strait of Georgia, and during July in southern Puget Sound. On the outside coast of Washington State pups are born in late April.

The salmon are often the most numerous and conspicuous species of fish in the Jade Coast estuaries, and all five species are present for part of their life cycles. The five species are sockeye, pink, coho, chinook, chum and steelhead. Salmon begin their lives as eggs laid in gravel nests known as "redds" shaped into the river bottom by spawning females. The males hover nearby to fertilize the eggs, which hatch into alevins. The tiny alevins remain in the gravel using a yolk sac for nourishment. They emerge from the gravel as fry to hunt tiny insects in the river. The fry become smolts when they leave the river for a life at sea. One to seven years later as adults, the salmon return to the stream to spawn. Although individual salmon fry linger for only brief periods in estuaries, some will double their size during their stay. This is a dangerous period in a salmon's life in which few fry survive. Critical to their success is rapid growth because large fish have far fewer predators than small fish. Estuaries provide a comparatively safe haven with an abundance of food relative to the open ocean. As adults, salmon enter estuaries where they adapt from seawater to freshwater before swimming upstream to spawn. Each species follows a different schedule so one or more species might be present in an estuary at one time of the year. Chinook diets comprise mostly insect larvae, pupae and adults that emerge from riverside marshes. Coho salmon fry follow a similar seasonal abundance pattern as chinook salmon. Common and red-breasted mergansers eat the eggs and fry of salmon. Common mergansers enter many of the small rivers in the Strait of Georgia when salmon are traveling to the sea in spring.[14]

THE LARGE CARNIVORES

My first encounter with Jade Coast grizzlies was along a salmon stream in southeast Alaska on a warm summer day. Anan Creek in southeast Alaska supports high densities of black bears and grizzlies when salmon return to spawn from June through October. It tumbles out of the mountains via the canyon and then slows to a snail's pace as it empties into a deep pool at the mouth. Salmon entering the creek must dart up the creek through shallow waters and the canyon where bears lie in wait.

Entering bear country is always an adrenaline-pumping experience and Anan Creek offers more than its share of thrills. The trail meanders along the creek edge and over treed ridges with limited visibility. Bears frequently walk the trail to seek out new fishing places along the creek so encounters are to be expected.

We had anchored our boat offshore and were preparing to walk the kilometer or two (about a mile) to a viewing point built by the U.S. Forest Service overlooking a canyon. I was in front of our group with bear spray at the ready and making plenty of noise to warn any bears of our presence. My eyes scanned the trail, then the slopes and finally came upon two grizzlies fishing in the river about 200 meters (650 feet) away. They were intent on catching fish, so I continued along the trail with my ears alert to any sounds up ahead. In about fifteen minutes I had arrived at the viewing platform above the creek, where three other people were already present. Below us were three black bears so full of salmon they could hardly move. Their black coats glistened in the sun.

The canyon was cast in shadow, but the sun shone brightly where the creek widened across a shallow gravel streambed above the canyon. In the sunlight, my eye caught the motion of a bear moving down the stream. A young grizzly had galloped into the water, trotted along a log and stopped at the top of the

Recycled Salmon

Black bears are frequent inhabitants of estuaries, where they live on berries, intertidal invertebrates and fish. An especially large sub-species of black bear, *Ursus americanus carlottae,* lives on a diet of marine invertebrates and fish on the Queen Charlotte Islands. Bears frequently hunt fish at night and take their prey into the forest to be eaten. Estimates put the total weight of salmon transported into the forest by an average bear at about 1,600 kilograms (3,520 pounds) per year. The nitrogen released from the decaying carcasses is recycled back into the growing trees, and the decaying trees release the nitrogen into the streams to be used by young salmon.[15]

canyon not more than 20 meters (65 feet) away. The sun shone on its brown muzzle as it sniffed the wind flowing up the canyon. I could see water droplets on the bear's face and see its sensitive nose move left and then right. I felt a momentary sense of vulnerability. I had already had two black bears not more than 5 meters (16 feet) away on the trail behind me. The only route I could see open to the grizzly would take it directly behind me and past the viewing plat-form. Without a moment's notice, the young grizzly plunged into the raging waters that would have swept a man off his feet, and walked to the far side of the river to disappear into dense rainforest undergrowth. At moments like this one feels most alive.

The large carnivores get most of their protein from fish, principally spawn-ing salmon. The killer whale enters estuaries in summer in pursuit of schools of salmon. Black and grizzly bears and bald eagles are lured to streams where salmon spawn. Both bear species have been extirpated from southern estuaries, but in parts of British Columbia and Alaska, the annual migrations of bears to streams continues each year. Knight Inlet and the Khutzeymateen River estuary in British Columbia, Anan Creek and Pack Creek in southeast Alaska, and McNeill River Sanctuary, Fish Creek and Brooks Camp in southern Alaska are some of the premier viewing places for grizzlies on the Pacific Coast. The bears move to these estuaries in spring to feed on the lush estuarine vegetation. They stay through summer to eat skunk cabbage roots, fern fiddleheads, and berries while awaiting the arrival of spawning salmon in autumn.

The carcasses of salmon drifting along spawning streams and into estuaries are scavenged by thousands of bald eagles through the winter. Especially large numbers of eagles gather in January near estuaries in the Squamish and Fraser rivers in British Columbia and the Skagit River in Washington. Over 10,000 chum salmon arrive in the Squamish River to find a mate, lay eggs and spawn in the gravel. Over 3,700 eagles from Alaska, British Columbia, Alberta and Montana converge on the river to scavenge the spent salmon carcasses. The eagles disperse along the Jade Coast to breed in March. Eagles mostly eat animals that they hunt or scavenge along beaches. Eagles in the Columbia River estuary spent 94 percent of their time perching in trees. They eat mostly large-scale suckers, American shad, common carp and peamouth but also took other fish, birds and mammals.

The impact of humans on the Jade Coast has been especially felt in the estuaries and lowlands where most of us reside. Those of us who are fortunate to live along the Jade Coast are blessed with one of the finest climates set in one of the most beautiful landscapes in the world. We are only beginning to understand and appreciate the interconnectedness of the bounty of living things and how far the connections reach beyond the Jade Coast. Some of those connections extend to distant lands and others reach into our souls.

Sunset, Sidney Island, British Columbia.

By the close of the twentieth century, two exceptionally intense El Niño events that heated the north Pacific Ocean subsided into a cool water La Niña phase. Over two decades earlier, scientists reported a major shift in the ocean ecosystem of the north Pacific. The effects of this regime shift and the two El Niño events were seen far and wide in the form of diminished salmon runs at spawning rivers, leatherback turtles in Alaskan waters, and mackerel and anchovies in fishing nets along the south coast of British Columbia.[1] Through all of this turmoil, the Pacific Ocean ecosystem harbored a diversity of species whose intricate lives and their ocean environment remain poorly known to science. Only recently have scientists begun to understand that the ocean regularly undergoes upheavals. Analysis of the depth of anchovy remains in sediments off the southern California coast confirms a close match between anchovy abundance and weather patterns going back three centuries. It is discoveries such as this that ignite the enthusiasm of scientists and also underscore how little we know about the ecology of the Jade Coast.

Some of the ideas expressed in this book will stand the test of time or falter as new information is gathered. But gradually we are beginning to better understand how the Jade Coast ecosystems function. The scientist in me anxiously awaits the new interpretations. I wonder how much we will know a century from now, and I lament that I will not live to read about it. In the meantime, I hope this book will excite young scientists, artists, musicians and poets to tell us new stories of the lives of the plants and animals that together make up the Jade Coast.

Glossary

Science has developed its own jargon. This glossary will help understand some of the important terms used by oceanographers and biologists.

Alevin—salmon eggs hatch into alevins, which remain in the gravel until they emerge as fry (see *fry, smolt* and *spawners*).

Amphipod—a shrimp-like crustacean.

Benthic—the seafloor.

Bloom—a sudden growth of plankton in spring and autumn that results in high concentrations.

Brackish—referring to seawater diluted by freshwater with a salinity of 0.5 to 17 percent.

Bysus—thread-like material produced by mussels to anchor to rocks.

Carnivore—meat eater, e.g., orcas, which eat salmon and marine mammals.

Continental shelf—the region of shallow water extending out to sea from the edge of continents.

Coriolis effect—an apparent force due to the rotation of the earth that acts perpendicular to the direction an object is moving. The effect is greatest near the poles and non-existent at the equator.

Crustacean—a large and diverse scientific grouping of animals that share features such as an external skeleton, a body divided into distinct sections, and jointed legs; e.g., crabs.

Diatom—A single-celled phytoplankton with overlapping silicate shells. These tiny plants are the most numerous organisms in the oceans.

Dinoflagellate—Mostly marine plants that are the most numerous of the plankton and have two whip-like tails called flagellae.

Ecosystem—the interaction of plants and animals with the environment.

Epiphyte—a plant that uses another species to support it in the water or air.

Euphausiid—a small shrimp that inhabits the oceans and is eaten by many fish, birds and whales.

Estuary—a region of seawater that is noticeably diluted by freshwater emanating from land. Estuaries form where rivers streams and creeks empty into the ocean. The high precipitation along the Jade Coast creates estuarine-like conditions near the shores of British Columbia and Alaska.

Food chain and food web—Terms for the interdependence of organisms as food items beginning with plants and ending with large carnivores. A food web can be thought of as a road map of food energy beginning with the sun's energy that is converted into chemical energy by plants and stored as sugars and starch, and ending with the largest carnivores. Along the route, the energy is passed between animals in their food. The food energy is used for activity, growth and reproduction or stored in their muscle and fat for future use. The players along the roadmap can be grouped by their activities in the food web such as the producers of energy, grazers and predators.

Fry—a young growth stage of salmon between the alevin and smolt stage (see *alevin*, *smolt* and *spawner*).

Habitat—the environment in which an organism resides. For example, the breeding habitat of a tufted puffin is grassy coastal headlands and islands with soil in which they can dig nesting burrows.

Herbivore—plant eater; e.g., sea urchins that eat kelp.

Intertidal zone—the region of beach exposed between the highest and lowest tide. Also known as the littoral zone.

Larva—the immature life stage of an animal.

Marsh—a wet vegetated area that is dominated by low-growing plants such as grasses, sedges and rushes. A saltmarsh is a marsh that grows along the seashore; an estuarine marsh grows at the mouths of rivers.

Mollusc—a soft-bodied animal with gills and a calcareous shell. The Mollusca family contains clams, snails, squids and octopii.

Mudflat—a predominantly mud beach.

Nutrient—chemical compounds required for growth by plants and animals.

Phytoplankton—Tiny floating plants that form the basis of most food webs in the oceans.

Plankton—tiny marine organisms with minimal swimming capacity that drift in the ocean currents.

Rainforest—a colloquial term referring to forests that grow in regions of the world with high levels of rainfall.

Rhizome—the underground root-like storage organ for plants.

Salinity—the salt content dissolved in seawater measured in parts per thousand.

Seabird—a colloquial term for birds that spend most of their lives at sea; puffins, albatross, cormorants and gulls are some well-known seabirds.

Seaduck—a colloquial term for ducks that spend some or all of their lives in saltwater; eiders and scoters are familiar seaducks.

Shorebird—a colloquial term for a diverse group of small to medium-sized birds that feed and nest near the shore; sandpipers, plovers and oystercatchers are familiar shorebirds.

Smolt—the stage at which salmon leave rivers and go to sea. Smolts are up to 12 centimeters (5 inches) in length (see fry).

Spawner—a reproductive adult salmon.

Tide—a cyclic flow of water generated by the forces of the moon and sun.

Trophosome—an organ packed with bacteria in deep sea tubeworms that absorbs carbon dioxide and oxygen from the seawater and hydrogen sulphide from the sea vent. The hydrogen sulphide is then shipped to the trophosome where the bacteria combine the oxygen into energy and produce a steady supply of sugars, fats and amino acids for the worms.

Upwelling—a term referring to the movement of water from the depths of the ocean to the surface. Upwelling is the result of the combined effect of wind, ocean currents, and spinning of the earth.

Zooplankton—tiny animals that form the plankton. Includes immature stages of jellyfish, worms, molluscs, crabs, snails and many other forms. Principal predators of the phytoplankton in the worlds' oceans and the basis of many food chains for fish, birds and mammals.

Endnotes

Many of the publications I reference in this book can be found in university libraries.

CHAPTER 1: LAND AND WATER

1. John Broadhead and Thom Henley, *Islands at the Edge* (Vancouver: Douglas and McIntyre, 1984) is a passionate plea for the protection of the Queen Charlotte Islands.

2. Robinson Jeffers, *Not Man Apart* (edited by David Brower, New York: Ballantine Books, 1969).

3. Jade is an aggregate mineral prized by the Chinese and Maori for thousands of years. It is very tough and hence useful as a tool. Nephrite jade has been known since ancient times and is found in British Columbia, whereas jadeite was identified in the sixteenth century in southeast Asia. Jade was shipped to China in coffins containing Chinese who died in British Columbia during the Gold Rush, and was more recently used to create the world's largest Buddha in a Bangkok monastery.

4. Philip Lambert compared the numbers of species of invertebrates and vertebrates occupying the coast of British Columbia to Atlantic Canada, Atlantic U.S.A., the British Isles and New Zealand. Although there were insufficient data to compare all invertebrate groups, British Columbia had the largest number of species in seven of the fourteen groups he compared ("Biodiversity of marine invertebrates in British Columbia" in *Biodiversity in British Columbia,* edited by Lee E. Harding and Emily McCullum, Ottawa: Canadian Wildlife Service, Ministry of Supply and Services, 1994, pp. 57–69). W. K. Fisher (*Asteroidea of the North Pacific and Adjacent Waters. Part 1. Phanerozonia and Spinulosa*. Volume 1. Washington, D.C., Smithsonian Institution, 1911) recorded 143 species of sea stars between San Diego and Point Barrow, Alaska, and Philip Lambert has identified sixty-nine species in British Columbia (P. Lambert, *The Seastars of British Columbia*. Victoria, B.C.: British Columbia Provincial Museum Handbook Number 39, 1981). Also see P. Lambert, "Range Extension for Some Pacific Coast Sea Stars (Echinodermata: Asteroidea)," *Canadian Field-Naturalist* 113: 667–69.

5. Rick Thomson's very readable book entitled *The Oceanography of the British Columbia Coast* (Ottawa: Canadian Special Publication of Fisheries and Aquatic (1981) provides excellent descriptions of tides and other oceanographic processes.

6. Kruckeberg, Arthur C. *The Natural History of Puget Sound Country*. Seattle: University of Washington, 1991.

7. Tom Carefoot provided photographic evidence of the uplifting effect of the 1965 earthquake in Prince William Sound in his book *Pacific Seashores* (Vancouver, B.C., 1977).

8. Hayes, D. *Historical Atlas of British Columbia, and the Pacific Northwest* (Delta, B.C.: Cavendish Books, 1999) summarizes information on Fousang and shows charts with references to the Pacific Northwest. The junk *Amoy* crossed the Pacific in 1922 and the *Keying* sailed halfway around the world, leaving Hong Kong on December 6, 1846, and reaching England on March 27, 1848.

9. B. G. Warner, R. W. Mathewes and J. J. Clague. "Ice-Free Conditions on the Queen Charlotte Islands, British Columbia, at the Height of Late Wisconsin Glaciation." *Science* 218 (1982): 75–77. Anthropologists believe that the first people to arrive on the coast came via an overland route through the interior of North America about 12,500 years ago or via the sea. The two hypotheses are described by Knut Fladmark in a paper entitled "Routes: Alternate Migration Corridors for Early Man in North America," *American Antiquity* 44 (1979): 55–6).

CHAPTER 2: COASTAL ECOLOGY

1. Jonathan Wiener's book *The Beak of the Finch* (Penguin, 1995) is a very readable and up-to-date review of current thought in evolution.

2. Thomas Carefoot. *Pacific Seashores*. Vancouver, B.C: J. J. Douglas, 1977.

3. Robert, M. May. *Stability and Complexity in Model Ecosystems*. (Princeton, New Jersey: Princeton University Press, 1973).

4. Terry Glavin's book *The Last Great Sea* (Vancouver: Greystone, 2000) provides an excellent summary of the impact of the Pacific fishery on the North Pacific ecosystem.

5. In 1979, British scientist James Lovelock published *Gaia: A New Look at Life on Earth* (Oxford University Press, 1979), in which he spelled out the Gaia Hypothesis. The hypothesis is that "the physical and chemical condition of the surface of the Earth, of the atmosphere, and of the oceans has been and is actively made fit and comfortable by the presence of life itself. This is in contrast to the conventional wisdom which held that life adapted to the planetary conditions as it and they evolved their separate ways." The Gaia Hypothesis posits that the living and inorganic material are part of a dynamic system that shapes the Earth's biosphere. Scientists generally agree that the Earth's ecosystem is maintained at a more or less steady state by the interactions of the living organisms with the nonliving components. However, there is not much acceptance for the view that evolution is the result of cooperative interactions as proposed by the Gaia hypothesis, rather than competitive processes as originally proposed by Charles Darwin.

6. The Russian crew was near Nevelsk-Sakhalin Island in the former U.S.S.R. celebrating

the 59th anniversary of the October Revolution of 1917 when they tossed a champagne bottle overboard with a message inside. It is on display in the Skidegate Museum in Skidegate, Queen Charlotte Islands.

CHAPTER 3: WEST TO THE WESTERLY WIND: THE OPEN OCEAN

1. Siegenthaler, U. and J. L. Sarmiento. "Atmospheric Carbon Dioxide and the Ocean," *Nature* 365 (1993): 119–25. Gerald A. Meehl and Warren M. Washington. "El Niño-like Climate Change in a Model with Increased Atmospheric CO_2 concentrations." *Nature* 382 (1996): 56–60.

2. There are several papers that have addressed climate change and weather effects on fish catches. Mysak, L. A., C. Groot, and K. Hamilton ("A Study of Climate and Fisheries: Interannual Variability of the Northeast Pacific Ocean and Its Influence on Homing Migration Routes of Sockeye Salmon." *Climatological Bulletin* 20 (1996): 26–35) examined the role of climate shifts, and Dick Beamish and Dan Bouillon at the Pacific Biological Station found that salmon catches were greater when low pressure weather systems prevailed in the North Pacific Ocean (see note 5 below). The opposite occurred when high pressure systems were present. Beamish and Bouillon believe that upwelling and hence productivity of the oceans increases during periods of low pressure. Cees Groot and Tom Quinn show a correlation between sea temperature and migration routes of salmon (see note 9 below). For a different view, see R. W. Tanasichuk's paper ("Implications of Interannual Variability in Euphausiid Population Biology for Fish Production along the South-West Coast of Vancouver Island: A Synthesis." *Fisheries Oceanography* 11 (2002): 18–30) in which he argues that variation in temperature, salinity and upwelling do not explain variations in the abundance of larval or adult euphausiids along the shores of Vancouver Island. He also points out that all fish do not respond to changes in plankton the same way.

3. Several authors have discussed that a regime shift occurred in the Pacific in the 1970s. The reader interested in this phenomenon is directed to papers by A. J. Miller and coworkers including "The 1976–1977 climate shift of the Pacific Ocean." (*Oceanography* 7 (1994): 21–26) and K. E. Trenberth and J. W. Hurrell's "Decadal atmosphere-ocean variations in the Pacific." (*Climate Dynamics* 9 (1994): 303–19). W. R. Shaw and his coworkers "Biological and species Interaction Survey of Pacific Hake, Sablefish, Spiny Dogfish and Pacific Herring off the Southwest Coast of Vancouver Island." (*Canadian Data Report of Fisheries and Aquatic Sciences* (1987) 651: 159) describe some of the biological effects of the regime shift on fish off British Columbia.

4. Heise, Kathy A. "Life History Parameters of the Pacific White-Sided Dolphin (Lagenorhynchus Obliquidens) and Its Diet and Occurrence in the Coastal Waters of British Columbia," MSc. thesis, Department of Zoology, University of British

Columbia, 1996. Robin Baird described the seasonality of whales in "Whales in Georgia Strait and Nearby Waters." (Vancouver Natural History Society, *Discovery* (1989) 18: 131–32). He also reviewed the status of the Pacific White-sided Dolphin in B.C. in "The Pacific White-sided Dolphin in British Columbia." (Vancouver Natural History Society, *Discovery* 20 (1991): 58–61 (includes refs.). Declines of common murres in fifteen of sixteen seabird colonies in Alaska between 1977 and 1992 were documented by John F. Piatt and P. Anderson in *the Exxon Valdez Oil Spill Symposium Proceedings of the American Fisheries Society, Symposium No. 18.* 1996, Bethseda, Maryland. Andrew W. Trites and Peter A. Larkin documented the declines of the sea lion in Alaska in a paper entitled "Changes in the Abundance of the Steller Sea Lions *(Eutopias Jubatus)* in Alaska from 1956 to 1992: How Many Were There?" *(Aquatic Mammals* 22 (1997): 153–66). David Rosen and Andrew Trites showed that captive sea lions lost weight when provided with unlimited pollack (*Canadian Journal of Zoology* 78 (2000): 1243–50).

5. Thomas Hayward wrote in an article entitled "Pacific Ocean Climate Change: Atmospheric Forcing, Ocean Circulation and Ecosystem Response," (*Trends in Ecology and Evolution* 12 (1997): 150–54,) that for 1,700 years the biomass of sardine and anchovy scales indicated periods of high and low abundance. He believed that these shifts indicated changes in ocean conditions over the last two millennia. In the North Pacific, zooplankton increased and salmon numbers decreased in the 1980s (Beamish, R. J. and D. R. Buillon. "Pacific Salmon Trends in Relation to Climate." *Canadian Journal of Fisheries and Aquatic Sciences* 50 (1993): 1002–16).

6. N. J. Aebischer, J. C. Coulson and J. M. Colebrook. "Parallel Long-Term Trends across Four Marine Trophic Levels and Weather." (*Nature* 347 (1992): 753–55).

7. Astrid Jarre-Teichmann, "The Potential Role of Mass Balance Models for the Management of Upwelling Ecosystems," (*Ecological Applications* 8 (1998): S93–S103) estimated the biological productivity of the major upwelling regions of the world. The Peruvian system produced about 65×10^6 kg.kilometers^2.yr^{-1}, compared to about 20×10^6 kg.kilometers^2.yr^{-1} in the Bengeula system and Northwest Africa systems, and 10×10^6 kg.kilometers^2.yr^{-1} in the California system.

8. Ware, D. M. and R. E. Thomson. "Link between Long-Term Variability in Upwelling and Fish Production in the Northeast Pacific Ocean." (*Canadian Journal of Fisheries and Aquatic Sciences* 48 (1991): 2296–306).

9. Cees Groot and Tom Quinn described the migration of salmon from the open ocean around Vancouver Island in relation to ocean temperature ("Homing Migration of Sockeye Salmon *Oncorhynchus nerka,* to the Fraser River." *Fishery Bulletin* 85 (1987): 455–69.) They showed that the proportions of salmon taking the northern and southern routes around Vancouver Island varied substantially between years. Between 1978 and 1985, the proportion of salmon along the northern route was positively correlated with sea temperatures off Vancouver

Island. It is likely that sea temperature affects the distribution of prey of the salmon, which then determines which route they will take.

10. Tsurumi, M. and V. Tunnicliffe. "Characteristis of a hydrothermal vent assemblage on a volcanically active segment of Juan de Fuca Ridge." *Canadian Journal of Fisheries and Aquatic Sciences* 58 (2001): 530–542.

11. Parsons, T. R., R. J. Brasseur, J. D. Fulton and O. D. Kennedy. "Production Studies in the Strait of Georgia, Part III." *Journal of Experimental Marine Biology and Ecology* 3 (1969): 39–50.

12. Mackas, D. and M. Galbraith. "Zooplankton on the West Coast Of Vancouver Island: Distribution and Availability to Marine Birds," pp. 15–21 in K. Vermeer, R. W. Butler and K. H. Morgan (eds.). *Status, Ecology and Conservation of Marine and Shoreline Birds on the West Coast of Vancouver Island*. Canadian Wildlife Service Occasional Paper Number 75, Ottawa, 1992. Richard Strickland describes the details of plankton life in his book *The Fertile Fjord: Plankton in Puget Sound* (Seattle: Puget Sound Books, 1983).

13. Chisholm, S. W. R., R. J. Olson, E. R. Zettler, R. Goericke, J. B. Waterbury and N. A. Welschmeyer. "A Novel Free-Living Prochlorophyte Abundant in the Oceanic Euphotic Zone." *Nature* 334 (1988): 340–43. Grassle, J. F. and N. J. Maciolek. "Deep-Sea Species Richness: Regional and Local Diversity Estimates from Quantitative Bottom Samples." (*American Naturalist* 139 (1992): 313–41).

14. James Clowater investigated the night-time foraging behaviour of western grebes in British Columbia where he found that bioluminescent plankton rising to near the sea surface at night fell prey to schools of young herring. The feeding actions of the fish left telltale clues that attracted grebes. "Distribution and foraging behaviour of wintering Western Grebes" (M.Sc. thesis, Simon Fraser University, Burnaby, B.C. 1998).

15. Jonathan Roughgarden, "How to Manage Fisheries," (*Ecological Applications* 8 (1998): S160–64).

16. Walker, M. W., J. L. Kirschvink, G. Ahmed, and A. E. Diction. "Evidence that Fin Whales Respond to the Geomagnetic Field During Migration." (*Journal of Experimental Biology* 171 (1992): 67–78).

17. Field, L. J. "Pacific Sandlance, Ammodytes hexapterus, with Notes on Related Ammodytes Species." Pp. 15–33 in N. J. Wilimovsky, L. S. Incze and S. J. Westrheim (eds.). *Species Synopses—Life Histories of Selected Fish and Shellfish of the Northeast Pacific and Bering Sea*. (Seattle: University of Washington Press, 1998.)

18. Healey, M. C. "Modelling the Coastal Migration of Juvenile Salmon through Hecate Strait, British Columbia." (*Canadian Technical Report of Fisheries and Aquatic Sciences* Number 1700, 1989). Estimates of fish abundance are understandably crude and variable from year to year.

19. The notion that juvenile salmonids in coastal waters are most numerous when their

arrival coincides with the peak abundance of plankton is known as the "match-mismatch" hypothesis originally developed by D. H. Cushing in a book entitled *Marine Ecology of Fishes* (London: Cambridge University Press, 1975). Carl Walters and his co-workers provided support for this hypothesis using data from salmon catches in B.C. (C. Walters, R. Hilborn, R. Peterman and M. Staley. "Model for Examining Early Ocean Limitation of Pacific Salmon Production." *Journal of the Fisheries Research Board of Canada* 35 (1978): 1303–15).

20. The number of seabirds estimated along the Pacific shores is presented in a monograph entitled "The Status, Ecology, and Conservation of Marine Birds of the North Pacific" (K. Vermeer, K. T. Briggs, K. H. Morgan and D. Siegel-Causey (eds.). *Canadian Wildlife Service Special Publication*, Ottawa, 1993). Terry R. Wahl, Ken H. Morgan and Kees Vermeer (*Seabird Distribution off British Columbia and Washington*, pp. 39–47) estimated 5,273,000 seabirds nested along the outer coast of British Columbia, and 211,302 off Washington's outer coast, W. B. Tyler, K. T. Briggs, D. B. Lewis and R. G. Ford (*Seabird Distribution and Abundance in Relation to Oceanographic Processes in the California Current System, pp. 48–60 ibid.*) estimated 940,900 nesting seabirds in Oregon and 544,700 off northern California.

21. There are estimated 2.3 million Cassin's auklets in British Columbia (see endnote 20). Kees Vermeer described the plankton diet, breeding chronology, growth of chicks and reproductive success of Cassin's Auklets in two papers he wrote ("The Importance of Plankton to Cassin's Auklets during the Breeding Season," *Journal of Plankton Research* 3 (1985): 315–29, and "The Diet and Food Consumption of Nestling Cassin's Auklets during the Summer and a Comparison with Other Plankton-Feeding Alcids." *Murrelet* 65 (1984): 65–77).

22. Tony Gaston describes in his delightful book, *The Ancient Murrelet* (London: T. & D. Poyser, 1992) the natural history of the ancient murrelet in the Queen Charlotte Islands. He used miniature transmitters attached to chicks and parents to estimate that the departure speed from nesting islands is in the order of about 2 to 3 kilometers per hour (1.3–1.9 mph). This is truly remarkable for a chick that weighs about 25 grams (0.8 oz) and has been out of the egg for only a few days. The few chicks that have been seen at sea were swimming alongside one or both parents.

23. Kaiser, G. W. and L. S. Forbes. "Climatic and Oceanographic Influences on Island Use in Four Burrow-Nesting Alcids." (*Ornis Scandinavica* 23 (1992): 1–6).

24. Details on whale foraging behaviour are available at an interactive web site developed by researchers Fred Sharpe and Larry Dill (www.sfu.ca/biology/berg/whale/abcwhale.html).

25. Baird, R. W., P. A. Abrams and L. M. Dill. "Possible Indirect Interactions between Transient and Resident Killer Whales: Implications for the Evolution of Foraging Specializations in the Genus Orcus." (*Oecologia* 89 (1992):125–32).

26. Hal Whitehead has written extensively on the social system of the sperm whale.

These articles include "Variation in the Feeding Success of Sperm Whales: Temporal Scale, Spatial Scale and Relationship to Migrations," (*Journal of Animal Ecology* 65 (1996):429–38) and "Babysitting, Dive Synchrony, and Indications of Alloparental Care in Sperm Whales," (*Behavioral Ecology and Sociobiology* (38 1989): 237–44). The analogy between whales and elephants was drawn by L. Wiegart, H. Whitehead and K. Payne in an article entitled "A Colossal Convergence" published in *American Scientist* 84 (1996): 278–87). See also Reeves, R. R. and H. Whitehead, "Status of the Sperm Whale, *Physeter macrocephalus*." (*Canadian Field-Naturalist* 111 (1997): 293–307).

27. Nathaniel Philbricks's riveting book *In the Heart of the Sea* (New York: Penguin, 2000) is a superb account of the sinking of the whaleship *Essex* by a sperm whale near the Society Islands on November 20, 1820, and the subsequent rescue of three crew near South America in February 1821. Philbrick's research provides insight into life onboard a whaleship, and the physiological and psychological toll of survival at sea. The whaler's reports indicated that the first encounter was an attack although others think it more likely an accidental collision. The second encounter was undisputedly an attack on the ship. Male sperm whales fight for access to females, and it is unlikely that a sperm whale would attack out of vengeance. The most likely interpretation is that the whale mistook the crew's hammering on the ship as clicking noises from another male sperm whale.

28. Rice, Dale W. "Sperm Whale" in S. H. Ridgway and R. Harrison (eds.) *Handbook of Marine Mammals*. Volume 4 (London: Academic Press, 1989). Parsons, T. R. "The Removal of Marine Predators by Fisheries and the Impact of Trophic Structure." (*Marine Pollution Bulletin* 25 (1992): 51–53).

29. Conway, K. W., Barrie, J. V., Austin, W. C. and Luternauer, J. L. "*Holocene* Sponge Bioherms on the Western Canadian Continental Shelf." (*Continental Shelf Research* 11 (1991): 771–90). Tunnicliffe, V. and C. M. R. Fowler. "Influence of Sea-Floor Spreading on the Global Hydrothermal Vent Fauna." (*Nature* 379 (1996): 531–33).

CHAPTER 4: ROCKY SHORES

1. Among the many scientists who have studied the ecology of rocky shores in the Pacific Coast, two giants in ecology are Robert Paine and Joseph Connell. Both scientists have produced classic studies in marine ecology. Paine coined the term "keystone species" to refer to usually predators that through their activities have a disproportionate effect on the presence of other animals (Paine, R. T. *Oecologia* 15 [1974]: 93–120). Two keystone species on rocky shores are the purple star (*Pisaster ochraceus*) and the sea otter (*Enhydra lutris*). With the experimental removal of the sea stars from rock shores, Paine showed that California mussels began to appear in deeper water where starfish formerly were found, and the mussels created a near monoculture by crowding out many other rocky shore species. Even more

celebrated is the example of the extirpation of the sea otter that resulted in a massive change to the rocky shore plant and animal communities. Joseph Connell's classic work was the research of zonation of plants and animals in the intertidal. Two influential papers were "The Influence of Interspecific Competition and Other Factors on the Distribution of the Barnacle *Chthamalus Stellatus*" published in *Ecology* 42 (1961): 710–23, and "Community Interactions on Marine Rocky Intertidal Shores" published in the *Annual Review of Ecology and Systematics* 3 (1972):169–92). Of the former paper, Tom Carefoot wrote in his book *Pacific Seashores* (Vancouver: J. J. Douglas, 1977) "Here, the ingredients were in the pot, Connell did the stirring, and ecologists were served up a conceptual *piece de resistance* that greatly influenced subsequent thinking and research on the whys and hows of shore zonation."

2. Ian McTaggart Cowan and Charles Guiguet reported in "The Mammals of British Columbia" (Victoria: B.C. Provincial Museum Handbook No. 11, 1956) that the last sea otter to be taken off the west coast of British Columbia was from Grassie Island near Kyuquot, British Columbia, in 1929. Eighty-nine otters were introduced to the region from Alaska between 1969 and 1972. The history and impact of the demise of the sea otter on the ecology of the rocky shore community is now well known. For readers wanting to know more about this story I suggest reading the popular account by Richard and Sydney Cannings, *British Columbia: A Natural History* (Vancouver: Greystone, 1996) or Edward O. Wilson's book *The Diversity of Life* (Cambridge, Massachusetts: Harvard University Press, 1992). A technical paper on the same subject was written by J. A. Estes and J. F. Palmisano entitled "Sea Otters: Their Role in Structuring Nearshore Communities" published in *Science* 185 (1974): 1058–60. *See also* Riedman M. L. and J. A. Estes. "The sea otter (Enhydra lutris): behavior, ecology, and natural history." *U.S. Fish and Wildlife Service Biological Report* 90 (14) (1990), Washington D.C. For the sea cow, I suggest reading L. Stejneger's paper entitled "How the Great Northern Sea-Cow (Rytina) Became Exterminated" published in *American Naturalist* 21 (1887): 1047–54 or D. P. Domning's monograph "*Sireniun* Evolution in the North Pacific Ocean" published by the University of California, Berkeley, Volume 118 (1978).

3. N. McDaniel "Life in the Fast Lane" (*Equinox* 41 (1988): 64–77).

4. J. R. E. Harger "The Effect of Wave Impact on Some Aspects of the Biology of Sea Mussels" publishes in the journal *Veliger* (12 (1970): 401–14) showed that the force required to remove shells of the surf-loving *Mytilus californianus* was far greater than the bay-living *Mytilus edulis*.

5. The classic study of barnacle bullying was done in Scotland by J. H. Connell in "*The* Influence of Interspecific Competition and Other Factors on the Distribution of the Barnacle *Chthamalus stellatus.*" (*Ecology* 42 (1961): 710–23).

6. Dayton, P. K. "Competition, Disturbance, and Community Organization: The

Provision and Subsequent Utilization of Space in a Rocky Intertidal Community." (*Ecological Monographs* 41 (1971): 351–89).

7. An excellent technical report detailing the food webs of the Strait of Juan de Fuca was written in 1979 by Charles Simenstad, B. Miller, C. Nyblade, K. Thornburgh and L. Bledsoe entitled "Food Web Relationships of Northern Puget Sound and the Strait of Juan de Fuca." (U.S. Environmental Protection Agency, EPA-600/7-79-259, Washington, D.C.). Copies are hard to locate but worth the search for anyone wishing to learn about linkages of major food webs.

8. T. Carefoot. *Pacific Seashores* (Vancouver: J. J. Douglas, 1977).

9 Eugene Kozloff, *Seashore Life of the Northern Pacific Coast* (Seattle: University of Washington Press, 1993) explained that the blue mussel, or bay mussel, as it is sometimes called, on the Pacific Coast has recently had a name change from *Mytilus edulis* to *Mytilus trossulus.* The former name had been reserved for the blue mussel living in the Atlantic Ocean.

10. P. K. Dayton. 'Experimental Evaluation of Ecological Dominance in Rocky Intertidal Algal Community. *Ecological Monographs* 45 (1975): 137–59.

11. E. F. Ricketts and J. Calvin provide a good description of tide pools and their inhabitants ("Between Pacific Tides." *Stanford University Press,* Stanford, California, 1968).

12. Bullock, T. H. 1953. "Predator recognition and escape response of some intertidal gastropods in the presence of starfish." *Behaviour* 5: 130–40; Margloin, A. S. "A running response of Acmaea to sea stars." *Ecology* 45 (1964): 191–93.

13. Behrens, S. "The Distribution and Abundance of the Intertidal *Prosobranchs Littorina scutulata* (Gould 1849) and *L. scutulata* (Phillipi 1845)," M.Sc. thesis (Vancouver: University of British Columbia, 1971.)

14. J. T. Wootton. "Indirect Effects, Prey Susceptibility, and Habitat Selection: Impacts of Birds on Limpets and Algae." *Ecology* 73 (1992): 981–91. Butler, R. W. and J. W Kirbyson. "Oyster Predation by the Black Oystercatcher." *Condor* (979) 81: 433–35.15. D. B. Irons, R. G. Anthony and J. A. Estes. "Foraging Strategies of Glaucous-Winged Gulls in a Rocky Intertidal Community." *Ecology* 67 (1992): 1460–74.

15. B. M. Leaman, "The Ecology of Fishes in British Columbia Kelp Beds, I. Barkey Sound Nereocystis beds." *Fisheries Development Report No. 22,* (Victoria: B.C. Ministry of Environment, 1980) showed that the abundance of fish declined following the removal of kelp canopy fronds in Barkley Sound. However, L. M. Moulton (below) found most rocky shore fishes in Puget Sound were not associated with kelp forests. L. M. Moulton, "An Ecological Analysis of Fishes Inhabiting the Rocky Nearshore Regions of Northern Puget Sound, Washington," Ph.D. thesis, (Seattle: University of Washington, 1977) provides a listing of the most abundant species and appendices that list prey items found in the stomachs of many rocky shore fish species in Puget Sound.

16. Hartwick, E. B., G. Thorarinsson and L. Tulloch. "Methods of Attack by Octopus dofleini (Wulker) on Captured Bivalve and Gastropod Prey". *Marine Behaviour and Physiology* 5 (1978): 193–200; and Hartwick, B., L. Tulloch and S. MacDonald. "Feeding and Growth of *Octopus dofleini* (Wulker)." *Veliger* 24 (1981): 129–38.

17. Kees Vermeer and Ron Ydenberg summarized the diet of seabirds and diving ducks on the Pacific Coast in a paper entitled "Feeding Ecology of Marine Birds in the Strait of Georgia" in *The Ecology and Status of Marine and Shoreline Birds in the Strait of Georgia, British Columbia* (K. Vermeer and R. W. Butler, eds., *Canadian Wildlife Service Special Publication*, Ottawa, 1989).

18. Sea otters found in Russia are the subspecies *Enhydra. lutris lutris* and those in Alaska are *E. lutris kenyoni*. The U.S. Fish and Wildlife Service and the U.S. Geological Survey reported that the Alaskan subspecies in the Aleutian Islands declined from as many as 100,000 otters in the 1970s to as few as 6,000 individuals by 2000. For an update on the status of the otter in British Columbia see Watson, J. C., G. M. Ellis, T. G. Smith and J. K. B. Ford. "Updated Status of the Sea Otter, *Enhydra lutris,* in Canada." *Canadian Field-Naturalist* 111 (1997): 277–86, and for background information see Riedman M. L. and J. A. Estes. "The Sea Otter (Enhydra lutris): Behavior, Ecology, and Natural History." *U.S. Fish and Wildlife Service Biological Report* 90 (14) (1990), Washington D.C.

19. LaCroix, D. L. "Foraging Impacts and Patterns of Wintering Surf Scoters on Bay Mussels in Coastal Strait of Georgia, British Columbia." M.Sc. thesis, Burnaby, B. C. Simon Fraser University, 2001.

20. Simenstad, C. A., J. A. Estes and K. W. Kenyon. "Aleuts, sea-otters, and alternate stable-state communities." *Science* 200 (1978): 403–09.

21. Ford, J. K. B., G. M. Ellis, and K. C. Balcomb. *Killer Whales.* (Vancouver, UBC Press, 1994).

22. Vermeer, K., K. H. Morgan, R.W. Butler, and G. E. J. Smith. "Population, Nesting Habitat, and Food of Bald Eagles in the Gulf Islands," pp. 123–30 in K. Vermeer and R. W. Butler (eds.) *The Ecology and Status of Marine and Shoreline Birds in the Strait of Georgia, British Columbia.* (Ottawa: Canadian Wildlife Service Special Publication, 1989).

23. M. A. Bigg. "Adaptations in the Breeding of the Harbour Seal, Phoca vitulina." *Journal of Reproduction and Fertility,* Supplement 19 (1973):131–42. T. M. Burge, A. W. Trites and M. J. Smith describe the genetic differences in populations of harbour seals in British Columbia and Alaska in their paper "Mitochondrail and Microsatellite DNA Analyses of Harbour Seal Population Structure in the Northeast Pacific Ocean" published in *Canadian Journal of Zoology* 77 (1999): 930–43.

CHAPTER 5: GRAVEL AND SAND

1. Eugene Kozloff's book *Seashore Life of the Northern Pacific Coast* (Seattle:

University of Washington Press, 1993) illustrates several of the small invertebrates that inhabit sandy shores.

2. Ibid.

3. Euell Gibbons, in his book *Stalking the Blue-Eyed Scallop* (New York: David McKay Company, 1964), tells an amusing way to capture the geoduck. He explains how the "neck man" dives to hold onto a retracting siphon that has given away its presence by ejecting a squirt of water. The "shovel man's" job is to dig furiously while the neck man's arm is slowly pulled by the siphon toward the clam buried many centimeters below the surface.

4. The Northwestern crow has been studied during its breeding season for over two decades by Nico Verbeek and his students, including me, in a series of papers and reviewed by Nico and me in the *Birds of North America,* Number 407 published in 1999 by the The Birds of North America, Inc., Philadelphia. The diet is described by me in a paper in the *Canadian Field-Naturalist* vol. 88 (1974): 313–16). Foraging behavior was described in a series of eloquent papers by Howie Richardson and his co-workers (*Journal of Animal Ecology* 54 (1985): 443–58; *Ecology* 67, (1985): 1219–26; *Ibis* 127 (1985): 174–83). Caching of clams was described in several papers by Paul James and Nico Verbeek (*Canadian Journal of Zoology* 75 (1985): 1351–56; *Behaviour* 85 (1983): 276–91, *Ardea* 72 (1984): 207–15), and the role of immature crows as nest helpers was described by Nico and me (*Ibis* 123 (1981): 183–89). [A review of the biology of the northwestern crow was written by Nico Verbeek and me (*Birds of North America No. 407,* The Birds of North America, Inc., Philadelphia, Pennsylvania, 1999).

5. Many gulls have black wingtips that resist wear. However, for unknown reasons some arctic breeding gulls have pale wing tips. Once explanation for pale wing tips in the glaucous-winged gull is that it is a feature left over from when the Pacific Coast was ice-covered more than 12,000 years ago.

6. John S. Oliver, P. N. Slattery, M. A. Silberstein and E. F. O'Connor. "Gray whale Feeding on Dense Ampeliscid Amphipod Communities near Bamfield, British Columbia," *Canadian Journal of Zoology* 62 (1984): 41–49.

7. John S. Oliver and P. N. Slattery. "Destruction and Opportunity on the Sea Floor: Effects of Gray Whale Feeding," *Ecology* 66 (1985):1965–75.

CHAPTER 6: EELGRASS MEADOWS AND SALTMARSH

1. The "rotten egg" smell in saltmarshes is produced by bacteria using sulfur as a terminal electron acceptor during sulfate reduction in the absence of oxygen.

2. R. C. Phillips estimated that about 9 percent of the bottom of Puget Sound was covered in eelgrass in his doctoral thesis "Ecological Life History of Zostera marina L. (Eelgrass) in Puget Sound, Washington" (Seattle: University of Washington, 1972).

3. F. T. Short showed how water temperature affected the production of eelgrass in a M.Sc. thesis entitled "Eelgrass Production in Charlestown Pond: An Ecological Analysis and Numerical Simulation Model" (Kingston: University of Rhode Island, 1975). Grant Hughes showed that gunnels moved into intertidal regions of southern Vancouver Island as the sea temperature rose in late winter. He published his results in a paper entitled "The Comparative Ecology and Evidence for Resource Partitioning in Two Pholidid Fishes *(Pisces: Pholididae)* from Southern British Columbia Eelgrass Beds." (*Canadian Journal of Zoology* 63 (1985): 76–85).

4. M. E. Kentula reported the weight of epiphytes was 2.3 times the weight of the eelgrass leaf in Netarts Bay in her doctoral thesis entitled "Production Dynamics of a *Zostera marina L.* Bed in Netarts Bay, Oregon" (Oregon State University, Corvalis, 1983). A brief description of the exchange of nutrients between eelgrass and their epiphytes is given by Ronald C. Phillips' technical review. M. M. Harlin provides an extensive list of the epiphytes and epifauna of eelgrass in a chapter entitled "Seagrass Epiphytes" in a book edited by R. C. Phillips and C. P. McRoy entitled *Handbook of Seagrass Biology: An Ecosystem Perspective* (New York: Garland Press, 1980). An easy-to-read description of some eelgrass epifauna, as well as many of the common animals of our coast, can be found in Eugene Kozloff's superb book *Seashore life of the Pacific Northwest* (Vancouver: Douglas and McIntyre).

5. For readers interested in a discussion of the role of microbes and nitrogen uptake in eelgrass, and the relationship of eelgrass and its associated ecosystem, I recommend the excellent technical review by Ronald C. Phillips, ibid. Danish studies of eelgrass ecosystems date from the beginning of this century and are referenced in R. C. Phillips's publication.

6. See J. R. Baldwin, J. R., and J. R. Lovvorn's paper entitled "Habitats and Tidal Accessibility of the Marine Foods of Dabbling Ducks and Brant in Boundary Bay, British Columbia." (*Marine Biology*, 120 (1994): 627–38. A study in the Netherlands showed that, over a year, birds consumed about 3.7 percent and invertebrates ate about 3.8 percent of the annual production of eelgrass (P. H. Nienhuis and A. M. Groenendijk. *Marine Ecology Progress Series* 29 (1986): 29–35).

7. The ecology of great blue herons on the British Columbia coast was written in a book by me entitled The Great Blue Heron. UBC Press, Vancouver: 1997).

8. The reader is referred to R. C. Phillips publication (above) and R. D. Bayer's paper entitled "Shallow-Water Intertidal Icthyofauna of the Yaquina Estuary, Oregon" (*Northwest Science* 55 (1981): 182–93) for a list of fish species recorded in eelgrass meadows. Doug Hay and his co-authors reviewed the distribution and abundance of small fish in the Strait of Georgia in a paper entitled "Distribution, Abundance and Habitat of Prey Fishes in the Strait of Georgia" published by Kees Vermeer and R. W. Butler ("*Status and Ecology of Marine and Shoreline Birds in the Strait of Georgia, British Columbia*" (Canadian Wildlife Service Special Publication, Ottawa,

1989). General natural history information on fishes is available in J. L. Hart's *Pacific Fishes of Canada* (Ottawa: Fisheries Research Board of Canada, 1973) and Andy Lamb and Phil Edgell's book *Coastal Fishes of the Pacific Northwest*, Pender Harbour, British Columbia: Harbour Publishing, 1986).

9. D. J. Townshend, P. J Dugan and M. W. Pienkowski reported on the territorial behavior of plovers in Britain in a chapter entitled "The Unsociable Plover—Use of Intertidal Areas by Grey Plovers" in P. R. Evans, J. D. Goss-Custard and W. G. Hale eds., *Coastal Waders and Wildfowl in Winter* (Cambridge University Press, 1984).

CHAPTER 7: ESTUARIES

1. Salinity of the Squamish estuary was reported by D. A. Levy and C. D. Levings in "A Description of the Fish Community of the Squamish River Estuary, British Columbia: Relative Abundance, Seasonal Changes, and Feeding Habits of Salmonids." (Fisheries and Marine Service, *Manuscript Report* 1475 (1978). Department of Fisheries and Oceans, West Vancouver, B.C.). The saltwedge in the Columbia River penetrates 42 kilometers (26 miles) upstream from its mouth, which is probably a record for Pacific Coast estuaries. In Grays Harbour, the saltwedge extends about 6.5 kilometers (4miles) upstream, and in the Fraser River it penetrates about 10 kilometers (6.3 miles) from the mouth.

2. John Davenport showed that lugworms timed periods of inactivity closely with low tides. The results were reported in his book *Environmental Stress and Behavioural Adaptation* (London: Croom Helm, 1985).

3. The sources of nitrogen and phosphorous can vary with the season. In the Columbia River, nitrogen was traced to river sources in winter, and, during summer, nitrogen and phosphorous was attributed to the ocean (Park et al., referenced by Charles Simenstad's book *The Ecology of Estuarine Channels of the Pacific Northwest Coast: A Community Profile* (U.S. Fish and Wildlife Service, Washington, D.C. USFWS/OB 83-05, 1983). It is highly likely that some nitrogen and phosphorous in our estuaries now originates from agricultural and forestry practices and municipal sewers.

4. Dissolved oxygen is an essential element in metabolism of anaerobic animals, and many decomposers compete for dissolved oxygen that is generally plentiful in estuaries because of mixing by currents and tides. Oxygen in Pacific estuaries is near saturation although Grays Harbour and Coos Bay have reported depletion in late summer and early autumn (Simenstad ibid).

5. Neil Dawe and Eric White describe the plant communities in two small estuaries in the Strait of Georgia ("Some Aspects of the Vegetation Ecology of the Nanoose-Bonell Estuary," *Canadian Journal of Botany* 64 (1986): 27–34), and Ian Hutchinson describes plant communities in the Fraser River estuary ("Vegetation-Environment Relations in a Brackish Marsh, Lulu Island, Richmond, B.C." *Canadian Journal of*

Botany 60 (1982): 452–62). J. M. Karagatzides estimated the average aboveground biomass in brackish marshes in British Columbia to be 880 to 2,300 grams per square meter (2 to 5 lbs per 10.7 square feet) for *Scirpus americanus* and 3,200 to 12,000 grams per square (7 to 26.5 lbs per 10.7 square feet)] for *Scirpus maritimus* ("Intraspecific variation of biomass and nutrient allocation in Scirpus americanus and Scirpus maritimus," M.Sc. thesis, Burnaby: Simon Fraser University, 1987). Ken Yamanaka estimated that the amount of aboveground biomass produced by marshes in the Fraser River estuary was about 2.5 times that of nearby farmland ("Primary Productivity of the Fraser River Delta Foreshore: Yield Estimates of Emergent Vegetation," MSc. thesis, Vancouver: University of British Columbia, 1975).

6. Root, T. *Atlas of Wintering Birds.* (Chicago: University of Chicago Press, 1998).

7. J. T. Carlton reviewed the impact of introduced species in estuaries of North America ("Introduced Marine and Estuarine Mollusks of North America: An End-of-the-20th-Century Perspective," *Journal of Shellfish Research* 11(2) (1992): 489–505).

8. John Baldwin and Jim Lovvorn reported the winter diet of wigeon, pintails and mallards in farmlands on the Fraser River delta in "The Abundance, Distribution and Conservation of Birds in the Vicinity of Boundary Bay" (R. W. Butler, (ed.). *Canadian Wildlife Service Technical Report Series* No. 155, Delta, B.C., 1992). The diet of wigeon was largely pasture and grass foliage, and wild seeds; whereas pintail ate mostly wild seeds, cabbage and insects; and mallards ate mostly wild seeds, corn, potatoes and cabbage.

9. Charles Simenstad provides an excellent review of the ecology of estuaries in his book *The Ecology of Estuarine Channels of the Pacific Northwest Coast: A Community Profile* (U.S. Fish and Wildlife Service, Washington, D.C. USFWS/OB 83-05, 1983).

10. E. O. Wilson's definition of a keystone species is "a species, such as the sea otter, that affects the survival and abundance of many other species in the community in which it lives. Its removal or addition results in a relatively significant shift in the composition of the community and sometimes even in the physical structure of the environment" (*The Diversity of Life.*" Cambridge, Massachusetts: Harvard/Belknap, 1992: p. 401).

11. Boyd, W. S. "Abundance Patterns of Trumpeter and Tundra Swans on the Fraser River Delta, B.C.," pp. 24–36 in R. W. Butler and K. Vermeer, eds. *The Abundance and Distribution of Waterbirds in Estuaries in the Strait of Georgia.* Canadian Wildlife Service Occasional Paper 83, Ottawa, 1994).

12. The Harrison's estimate of bacteria on eelgrass detritus was reported in K. R. Tneore and B. C. Coull (eds.) *Marine Benthic Dynamics* (Columbia, South Carolina: University of South Carolina Press, 1980).

13. Gordon, D. K. and C. D Levings (*Seasonal Changes of Inshore Fish Populations on Sturgeon and Roberts Banks, Fraser River Estuary, British Columbia.* (Canadian Technical Report of Fisheries and Aquatic Science 1240. Department of Fisheries and Oceans, Vancouver, B.C., 1984) is an excellent technical review of the occurrence and abundance of fish in a large Pacific estuary. For information on salmon see Cees Groot and Leo Mangolis' book "Pacific Salmon Life Histories" (Vancouver, UBC Press, 1991).

14. The behavior of common mergansers preying on juvenile salmon appeared in papers by C. C. Wood (*Journal of Fisheries and Aquatic Science* 42985: 1259–71, *Canadian Journal of Zoology* 63 (1985): 1260–70) and C. C. Wood and C. M. Hand (*Canadian Journal of Zoology* 63985: 1271–79).

15. The results of isotope analysis of trees and shrubs near streams that showed that nearly one-quarter of the nitrogen in their leaves was derived from spawning salmon was published in a paper in 2001 by James Helfield and Robert Naiman entitled "Effects of Salmon-Derived Nitrogen on Riparian Forest Growth and Implications for Stream Productivity" (*Ecology* 82: 2403–09). Tom Reimchen's work on the connection between spawning salmon, bears and the forest was published in an account written by Nancy Baron entitled "Salmon Trees" published in *Canadian Geographic* (April/May 2000): 51–59. Nancy explained how Tom measured the nitrogen 14 and 15 isotopes ratios in augered cores from old trees. Nitrogen 14 is derived from air, and nitrogen 15 is from the marine environment. The results showed the nitrogen 15 signal in tree cores, indicating a long period of marine contribution to the trees' growth. An interesting aside was that the signal increased sometime about 1900, which coincided with an abandonment of a Haida village there following a smallpox outbreak. Presumably the presence of the Haida dissuaded bears from using the stream to forage for fish.

EPILOGUE

1. Terry Glavin's book *The Last Great Sea* (Vancouver: Greystone, 2000) is an excellent lucid portrayal of many conservation issues facing the north Pacific Ocean. Carl Safina's *Song for the Blue Ocean* (New York: Henry Holt and Company, 1997) is an eloquent and passionate plea to preserve the oceans. For a technical review of conservation measures for the world's oceans, see Eliott Norse's *Global Marine Biological Diversity* (Washington D.C.: Island Press, 1993) or Boyce Thorne-Miller's *The Living Ocean: Understanding and Protecting Marine Biodiversity* (Washington D.C.: Island Press, 1999).

Acknowledgments

It has taken years of research by many dedicated scientists working these waters to piece together the story of the Jade Coast. With immense respect, I tip my hat to all of them. In many ways, this is their book. I have synthesized their results to develop the connections that form the basis of this book; any errors in the interpretation of their results are my own.

Many people have helped me while writing this book. I reserve special gratitude to Sharon Butler, Holly and Tom Middleton, Myrica Butler and James Butler Cairns for their patience while I wrote this book and for sharing their enjoyment of the seashore. I thank Randy Burke for his friendship and for the opportunity to visit many out-of-the-way places along the coasts of British Columbia and Alaska onboard the *Island Roamer*. His seamanship and frienship are rare commodities that I greatly value. I also thank the crew of the *Island Roamer*—Louis Rzen, Jan Bevelander, Cathy Burke, Cindi Cowie, Rick Crosby, Jane Fearing, Bev Ford, Pat Gerlach, Ian Giles, Peter Heiberg, Iain Jones, Pat Murray, Jim Mattson, Kate Riddell, Tom Steere and Chris Tullock— who made the trips so pleasant. Mark Hobson, Danny Kent and Austin Reed allowed me to publish some of their superb photos.

The Canadian Wildlife Service and the Brisith Columbia Parks provided me many opportunities to study along the Pacific Coast during regular employment. Prominent among members of these agencies were my colleagues Bob Elner, Moira Lemon and David Stirling. Many people generously shared their knowledge of the coast or commented on parts of this book. Bob Elner read the entire manuscript, Cynthia Durance shared her knowledge of eelgrass ecosystems, and Kitty Lloyd provided her knowledge of rocky shores. Doug Bertram, Sean Boyd, Randy Burke, Wayne Campbell, Myke Chutter, Pete Clarkson, Fred Cooke, Jim Darling, Michael Dunn, John Elliott, Bob Elner, John Ford, Ruth Foster, Ian Goudie, Mark Hobson, Lee Harding, Stephanie Hazlitt, Kathy Heise, Danny Kent, Glen Jamieson, Debbie Lacroix. Colin Levings, Moira Lemon, Rod MacVicar, Jeff Marliave, Terry Sullivan, Terry Sutherland and Ron Ydenberg contributed information.

I am especially grateful to Anna Porter who took time out on a sunny afternoon on a remote beach in the Queen Charlotte Islands to read the manscript and to Michael Mouland at Key Porter who guided the project.

Appendix

Table 1. Estimated number of breeding seabirds on the Jade Coast. The estimates are in summary papers written by seabirds scientists and published in 1993 in a special publication of the Canadian Wildlife Service entitled *The status, ecology, and conservation of marine birds of the North Pacific* and edited by Kees Vermeer, Kenneth T. Briggs, Ken H. Morgan and Douglas Siegel-Causey.

Species	Alaska	British Columbia	Washington/Oregon	California
Northern fulmar	150	4	0	0
Leach's storm-petrel	3.5–6.8 million	1.1–2.2 million	400,000	20,000
Fork-tailed storm-petrel	3–5 million	300,000–1.3 million	5,000	0
Brandt's cormorant	0	150	16,600	65,000
Double-crested cormorant	100	4,000	5,700	2,000
Pelagic cormorant	1,100	8,400	12,000	16,000
Glaucous-winged gull	266,000	58,000	29,000	0
Western gull	0	0	15,000	51,000
Herring gull	100	0	0	0
Ring-billed gull	0	0	106	0
Mew gull	15,000	0	0	0
Pigeon guillemot	40,000	10,200	22,360[b]	
Marbled murrelet	250,000–1 million	50,000	8–12,000[b]	
Kittlitz's murrelet	25,000–100,000	0	0	0
Common murre	10,000[a]	6,000	457,000	363,000
Rhinoceros auklet	110,000	446,000	62,000	2,000
Tufted puffin	97,000	77,000	28,000	1,000
Ancient murrelet	60,000	523,000	0	0
Cassin's auklet	250,000	2.8 million	55,000	59,000

[a] Estimate for southeast Alaska; [b] combined estimate for Washington, Oregon and California

Table 2. Relative abundance of the most common seabirds in summer in the eastern north Pacific. The estimates were published in a paper entitled *Marine birds and mammals of the Pacific subarctic gyre* published in 1999 in *Progress in Oceanography* volume 43, pages 443-487 by A. M. Springer, J. F. Piatt, V. P. Shuntov, G. B. van Vliet, V. L. Vladimirov, A. E. Kuzin and A. S. Perlov.

Species name	Relative abundance	Species name	Relative abundance
Black-footed albatross	10,000	Other storm petrels	2,100
Laysan albatross	78	Red phalarope	6
Northern fulmar	7,200	Gulls	660
Shearwaters	47,000	Black-legged kittiwake	1,200
Buller's shearwater	18	Murres	42
Gadfly petrels	2,800	Tufted Puffin	700
Fork-tailed storm-petrel	4,400	Horned Puffin	38
Leach's storm-petrel	4,900		

Table 3. Estimated number of marine mammals on the Jade Coast. Unless otherwise stated, estimates of mammals were taken from Don E. Wilson and Sue Ruff's book *The Smithsonian Book of North American Mammals* published in 1999 by the University of British Columbia Press, Vancouver.

Species	Number	Species	Number
Sea otter	100,000	Pacific white-sided dolphin	900,000–1 million
Northern fur seal	10,200	Risso's dolphin (CA to WA)	32,000
Steller's sea lion	116,000	False killer whale	Unknown
California sea lion (CA to WA)	33,000[a]	Short-finned pilot whale	Widespread but unkown
Harbour seal	285,000		
Northern elephant seal	125,000	Unknown Killer whale	1400[c]
Minke whale (northwest Pacific)	25,000b	Northern right whale dolphin	Unknown
Sei whale	14,000	Harbor porpoise	Widespread but no data
Blue whale	1,400–1,900	Dall's porpoise	1.1 million
Fin whale	Widespread but unknown	Sperm whale	930,000
Gray whale	21,000	Dwarf sperm whale	Unknown

[a] NOAA-NWFSC Technical Memo 28 (1997); [b] International Whaling Commission; [c] John Ford, Dept. Fish. & Oceans, Canada, personal communication

Index